Coats Family
1933-1994 and After

Coats Family
1933-1994 and After

Deane Dierksen

**WITH MANY COMMENTS FROM SIBLINGS:
DONNA SEVILLA, DAVID COATS, AND DOUGLAS COATS.**

Genealogy House
Amherst, Massachusetts

Published 2021 by Genealogy House,
a division of White River Press, Amherst, Massachusetts
www.genealogyhouse.net

ISBN: 978-1-887043-98-4

Book and cover design by Douglas Lufkin
Lufkin Graphic Designs, Norwich, Vermont
www.LufkinGraphics.com

Cover Photos:
Front:
     On the left, Ouida and Bill shortly after their marriage in 1933.
     On the right, Bill and Ouida about 1979

Back, clockwise from the left:
1.   In the back: Bill with baby Donna, Deane, Ouida; in front David and Doug — July 1950
2.   In the back: David and Doug; in front Deane and Donna — June 1951
3.   From L to R: Deane, Doug, Donna, Ouida, David, Bill — April 1957
4.   Standing: Deane, Donna, David, Kathy, Doug, Helen. Seated: Ouida, Bill — September 1981 Coats family reunion

Preface

OVER THE YEARS, I have written down some of my memories and solicited comments from my siblings, David, Doug, and Donna. Several times we had an email round robin going. File dates range from 1990s almost to the present. Some information came from my research, some came from the large collection of letters that my cousin Sandra (Moulton) Burridge sent me in the summer of 2004 and from another collection from Victoria (Moulton) Whittall in March 2009. Both sets of letters were written by my mother, Ouida; her two siblings, Irene Adermann and Jasper Moulton; and their mother, Bess Moulton, in the 1960s and 1970s, as well as one letter by Bess in 1946.

I was also fortunate to acquire two small collections of Ouida's family Christmas newsletters, which have scattered dates from 1958-1980. The newsletters provided dates, places, and other useful bits of information; Donna had a photo album in which four early ones (1958-1961) were pasted. Six later ones came from Betty Paris Brown, the widow of my father's first cousin Clair Edward Paris. I met Betty in Manchester, Iowa, in September 2001, where she showed me around Delaware County, shared family information, and took me to family cemeteries. While there I also visited the county courthouse to get other family information; I was standing in the tiny deed room when the news broke about 9/11.

The address compilation started with a list my mother typed about 1961 of the towns she and my father had lived in since their marriage in June 1933, based on their recollections. In

2001, David sent me a copy of a document in my mother's handwriting that he had from about the same time; perhaps it was the basis for the list I have, as it added several street addresses. Perhaps my mother had started the list when I needed a to provide all of my addresses since 1 January 1937 (practically my whole life) for a security clearance when I was working for the Army, which I did from 1961 to 1964. David may have needed the information also.

The content of this book was last updated on 3 December 2020, at 8:22 p.m.

Deane Dierksen
December 2020

FATHER

Louis David "Bill" Coats (1910-1994) was the third of the eight children of Ernest Leslie "Chub" Coats (1881-1948) and Verona Jane Paris (1884-1924). His parents were both born and grew up in Delaware County, Iowa, and moved to Spink County, South Dakota, in early 1907. His mother taught school before her marriage. Bill was born on his parents' farm near Doland, South Dakota, in 1910 and was the first member of his family to finish high school.

Baby Bill Coats, 1910.

Mother

Ouida Sturges Moulton (1913-1982) was the second of the three children of Royal Jasper (R. J.) Moulton (1879-1952) and Bessie Ellen (Bess) Sturges (1885-1971). Ouida was born in Fulda, Minnesota, where her father was the principal of the local high school. She lived most of her childhood years in Cando, North Dakota, population 1,111 in 1920. There her father was superintendent of schools and her mother taught eighth grade. Ouida graduated from Cando High School in 1930. In the fall of that year, the family moved to Huron, South Dakota, where her father joined the faculty of Huron College.[1]

Baby Ouida Moulton, 1913.

Ouida - 1928

Ouida at age 15.

---

1   For more about Ouida's childhood, see my article, "Moulton Family Life in Cando, North Dakota, 1920-1930," *Minnesota Genealogist* 43, no. 1 (Spring 2012): 13-19.

THEIR CHILDREN

Bill and Ouida had four children, two girls and two boys:

1. **Deane Moulton Coats**, born 21 April 1936 in Huron, married 26 August 1961, Alan Parker Dierksen (1931-2006), and divorced in 1984. They had two children.

2. **Louis David Coats**, born 1 October 1939 in Pierre, South Dakota, married 8 January 1972, Katherine "Kathy" Howlett (1944-2020). David adopted Kathy's two children from a previous marriage. He has always been called Dave or David.

3. **Douglas Ernest Coats**, born 2 November 1941 in St. Paul, Minnesota, married (1) 1967, Helen Anne Selleck, divorced ca. 1982; married (2) 9 November 1986, Manerat "Lee" Vongsermsin, had two daughters, and divorced ca. 2007; married (3) 12 April 2019, Judith Carol Epstein.

4. **Donna Ellen Coats**, born 30 September 1949 in Estherville, Iowa, married 27 May 1971, Charles Martin Sevilla. Donna had one daughter from a previous relationship.

ABOUT BILL

Our father was always called Bill; I have never discovered why. His usual signature and directory entry was: L. D. "Bill" Coats.

Bill, his sister, and six brothers attended a one-room country school through eighth grade. After finishing the eighth grade, Bill stayed out of school for about two years. He didn't work much on the home farm then, but he worked some for Swift & Company at its cream station in Doland. For at least one harvest season, he worked for a farmer who used old-fashioned methods. It was very hard work and the only break he would get was when they moved the tractor. (This information was shared by Bill's brother Maurice "Sid" Coats in August 1998 at a Coats' family reunion.)

1921 school group, from a small original, in poor shape, owned by M. E. (Sid) Coats. This image has been professionally repaired. The school was located south of Doland at a cross-roads about 1/4 mile from the farmhouse where the Coats family was then living. Identification by Sid, August 1999. Back: Louis & Norma Coats, Dorothy Haas, Warren Wolverton. Front: unknown, Howard & Sid Coats, Walter Haas, Marion Wolverton, Guy Steely, unknown.

Bill in his football helmet, 1929.

Bill then attended Doland High School where he played football, baseball, basketball, and track—and earned letters in all of them. His brother Sid said that track and football were Bill's best sports. At one point he had a record in high hurdles that stood for some years. He placed second in the state in high hurdles at a time when all schools competed together and there was no separation between large and small schools. Someone from a larger school won first. (This information came via telecon with "Sid" Coats on 5 July 1992).

Athletics continued to play a big part throughout his life and sometimes determined how family life was organized. When I was a child he played golf whenever the weather permitted, bowled in a league (or two) at least several winter seasons, and managed an amateur softball team for at least one summer in Perry, Iowa. He did not like the water or water sports; he continued to play golf until he was about 80.

After his high school graduation in 1930, Bill went to work for Swift & Company. In his early days with the company, he drove a truck, picked up eggs and cream from farmers, and did various other kinds of work in their operation. He was sent to a lot of small towns around the area (as per telecon with "Sid" Coats 5 July 1992). Ouida said that Bill was sometimes transferred every month or two, often with little or no notice.

About Ouida

Throughout her life Ouida loved the water and swimming. An excellent swimmer, she could still do jackknife and swan dives late in her life. She could also lie on top of the water and float seemingly indefinitely without moving her hands and feet, something none of her children could do. Her best swimming stroke—Australian crawl, as it was then called—was not fast, but smooth and even with a breath with every stroke. It looked as if she could swim for hours.

At some point in her life, Ouida developed a desire to travel. I am not sure when this started, but apparently it was a long-standing wish. It wasn't until middle age that she had the opportunity to do it. She didn't leave accounts of her travels, but we do know where in general she went and in what year. Donna and Doug inherited her love of travel.

Ouida was a lifelong reader. When she was a child, her parents, both educators, encouraged her and her siblings to read the classics. She encouraged me to read them, too. When I was a child I remember she read lots of mysteries and magazines as well as other types of fiction and some nonfiction. During the period when the family moved a lot, she always said that when she had read all the mysteries in the library it was time to move.

She finished three years at Huron College and later said several things motivated her to get married before she got her degree. Bill's sudden transfer from Huron was perhaps the major factor. Her parents' move to Pierre in 1933 was another factor; her father had taken a position there with the South Dakota State Department of Education because Huron College was no longer paying its faculty or was paying in scrip. Also, Ouida's sister, Irene, a 1932 Huron College graduate, was doing babysitting for something like $7.50 per week because it was the only job she could find—a fact that made finishing college seem less worthwhile.

Ouida diving, 1931.

The Moulton family in 1932, left to right:
R. J., Ouida, Bess, Irene, and Jasper.

7

COURTSHIP AND MARRIAGE

We don't know how Bill and Ouida met. She was in Huron so he must have been in that vicinity in 1932-1933. David said he asked Ouida several times where they met, and she said she wouldn't tell him. None of the rest of us remembers ever hearing anything about it. Perhaps they met at dances. Ouida did talk about how much she enjoyed the frequent dances held in the area, but not who she was with. We also heard that Lawrence Welk's band played frequently and was not considered special then. Sometimes a crowd went in one car and the women had to sit on the men's laps in the car so everybody could fit in.

The couple married at her parents' home in Huron, South Dakota, on 18 June 1933. Her parents gave them the choice of having a large wedding or a small home wedding plus money to set up housekeeping and buy furniture. They chose the small wedding.

Bill and Ouida's wedding notice as it appeared in the Willow Lake [S.D.] News.

Their wedding day, 18 June 1933; left to right: Ouida's brother, Jasper; L. D. Coats—the groom; Ouida; and Norma Coats, Bill's sister.

Ouida's maternal grandfather, A. E. Sturges, sent a letter that included this advice on marriage:

> You sure have picked a lean time to start on the journey of life as housekeeper and manager of a new home.
>
> All this may be an advantage however if it is viewed from the right angle, as your neighbors will not be expecting quite as much from you as they would if times were booming.
>
> You can keep down running expenses without exciting comment and in many ways use the times to advantage. You certainly got us at a time when new tin looks like silver, all the same I have eaten many a good meal on a tin plate and used a tin cup for coffee, and have stood it for over fifty one years, and knowing the stock you came from I have every confidence that you will make good and will be able to do your part towards the keeping of the new home in order.
>
> Make the best of what you have and in due time as conditions change you will be able to look back to the beginning with pride and a strength that only comes from a success won under such trying conditions.

(Letter dated 15 June 1933; a copy is in my files.)

The Family Story, Told by Location

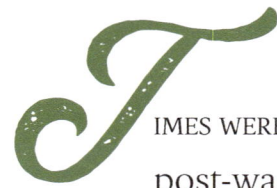

*T*IMES WERE HARD IN THE DAKOTAS in the 1920s and 1930s, beginning with post-war deflation in the 1920s, the depression beginning in 1929, and droughts in 1933-1934.[2] All of the family must have been affected by the dust storms that affected wide areas, including the Dakotas. The Huron weather station noted that the "number of days with dust storms that involved practically the entire State was 60 for the 5-month period, January to May 1934." One of the worst storms occurred from April 18-23 when "Dust storms continued to prevail with great severity." On the 21st "the storm was so severe that darkness came on at 4:36 p.m. and continued until 5:56 p.m. during which time lights were required. Visibility was reduced to only 50 feet."[3]

Ouida's father not only left his job in Huron because of the inability of the college to pay his salary; he had previously moved the family from Cando in 1930 when the school system there could no longer pay his full salary. On top of that, Ouida's grandfather, Jasper Moulton, lost money in a bank failure, and Bill's father was living on a rental farm by 1930, having sold his farm in 1929 for $1 and "other considerations," which may have meant payment of his debts.

After Bill and Ouida's marriage, Swift & Company continued to transfer Bill frequently. Little is known about their first homes except that they had very little money. The good news was that Bill always had a job, which many didn't during the depression. Ouida

---

2 Herbert S. Schell, *History of South Dakota*, 4th ed., rev. (Pierre, S.D.: South Dakota State Historical Society Press, 2004), 277-297.

3 W. A. Mattice, U.S. Weather Bureau, Washington, D.C., "Dust Storms, November 1933 to May 1934," *Monthly Weather Review* (February 1935): 53. Viewed 23 May 2020 at ftp.library.nooa.gov.

remembered that they ate whatever they had left the day before payday, no matter how strange the combination. She also said that they had a lot of fun then, despite their lack of money. As far as we know, Ouida did not work during this period. There were probably no jobs for her, especially with their frequent moves.

WILLOW LAKE, SOUTH DAKOTA
JUNE–SEPTEMBER 1933

Bill and Ouida's first home after their marriage was in Willow Lake. At that time Bill managed the Swift Produce Branch there.[4]

HURON, SOUTH DAKOTA
SEPTEMBER 1933–AUGUST 1934

On 30/31 August 1933, Ouida took the Red Cross Life Saving Examiner test in Huron. She passed the two-day test, and she earned a swimsuit patch that she kept for the rest of her life. The local newspaper described the test.

According to the *Evening Huronite*:

> Methods which the applicants would use in teaching swimming and life saving were emphasized in the tests. All candidates were reviewed on breaking strangle holds, correct approach and correct carrying methods in life saving.

> When Mr. Eaton's recommendations are formally approved by the American Red Cross, the successful applicants will be eligible to give official Red Cross swimming and life saving tests.

> An examiner's certificate is the best recommendation a person can have in applying for a position of life guard.[5]

The Red Cross patch that Ouida earned.

---

4   *Willow Lake* [S.D.] *News*, 6 June 1933, p. 1, c. 6.

5   "5 Pass Red Cross Life Saving Tests," *Evening Huronite* [Huron, S.D.], 31 August 1933, p. 5, c. 1.

We do not know whether Ouida ever served as a lifeguard or taught Red Cross swimming classes. For many years, Red Cross certification was required to become a lifeguard.

The following year, the *Evening Huronite* reported the following:

> Mr. and Mrs. William [sic] Coats left for Aberdeen to make their home. Mr. Coats was transferred there by Swift and company to have charge of the poultry feeding operation there. Mrs. Coats was formerly Miss Ouida Moulton of Huron.[6]

ABERDEEN, SOUTH DAKOTA
AUGUST 1934-JANUARY 1935

Though there is no further information, from data that gives his job titles, it seems that Bill was learning about many facets of the poultry business.

HURON, SOUTH DAKOTA
JANUARY 1935-MAY 1937

This is the city where I was born on 21 April 1936.

- **675 Beach.** This was my parents' address in the undated 1935 South Dakota State Census. At that time, the estimated population of Huron was 12,123.

- **803 Beach Avenue, S. E.** This address is per the 1936 Huron City Directory. By this time, Bill was an assistant manager at the local Swift & Company plant. My birth certificate says he was assistant manager, sales division. Donna and I drove by the house in August 1999; it was a fairly large frame house of at least two floors and had an outside stairway to the second floor. Perhaps Bill and Ouida lived in that apartment.

- **441 Simmons, S.E.**, as of 24 November 1936.

Bill and Ouida with me— baby Deane—in 1936.

6 *Evening Huronite*, 7 August 1934, p. 5, c. 4.

- **206 South 5th**. Ouida's father, Roy Moulton, liked information on the family tree and photos of the generations. In the fall of 1938, he wrote that he "took Ouida, Deanne [sic], and myself to Mankato and had a four generation picture taken, with dad [Jasper Moulton], and he seemed very pleased with it." (Letter to his sister, Dora Moulton Balano, 24 October 1938, a copy of which is in my files.) *(Note: My grandfather Moulton thought my name should have been* Deanne—*with two "n's"—and he always spelled it that way. I wish his preference had prevailed, as it's a more common spelling. DD)*

We have little information on the family in Montevideo until the family was about to move. On 2 September 1939, an item in the local news section of the *Montevideo News* noted: "Mr. and Mrs. L. D. Coates and daughter Deane are moving this week to Detroit Lakes. They have resided here for two and one-half years, Mr. Coates having been assistant manager of the Swift & Company plant here. He spent Tuesday in Detroit Lakes, and they plan to move there either today or Friday."

At that time Ouida was pregnant and near term with David. She said Bill asked Swift to postpone the move till after the baby was born, but he was told to move or lose his job. He went to Detroit Lakes, and my mother and I went to her parents' home in Pierre where David was subsequently born in the Catholic hospital on 1 October 1939. Ouida said Bill never forgave Swift for this, and he left the company as soon as he could.

I have little memory of the towns before St. Paul. In one of them—probably Montevideo because it is on a river—my mother remembered not being able to find me for long enough that the authorities were getting ready to drag the river. It turned out that a neighbor man had taken me me on an outing with his children but did not let Ouida know. That got him in big trouble with his wife, or so the story goes.

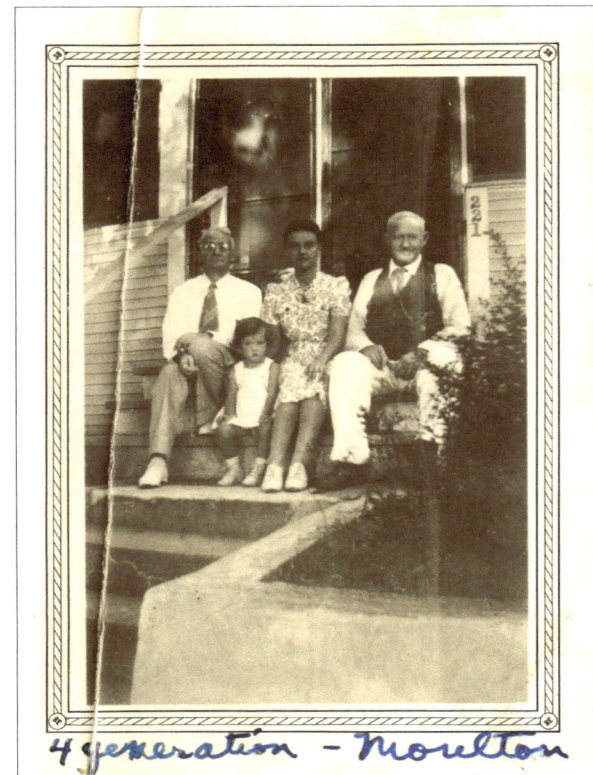

Four generations of Moultons, left to right: R. J. Moulton, Ouida Coats, Jasper Moulton, and Deane sitting on the steps.

About my only other memories of this time are sitting on Ouida's lap at an evening movie and when Bill came to get us at our Moulton grandparents' home. That happened on two occasions. The first was in the late summer or early fall of 1937. My mother and I were there after my grandmother suffered a skull fracture in a fall down her basement stairs and was in critical condition.[7] Ouida was the only family member who could come take care of her. More likely it was when my father came to get us fall 1939, after David was born. [I am more likely to remember this at 3 than at one.]

DETROIT LAKES, MINNESOTA
SEPTEMBER 1939-AUGUST 1940

Louis David Coats Jr., who was simply called "David," was born in Pierre on 1 October 1939.

Bill had moved to Detroit Lakes shortly after 10 September. Ouida, Deane, and baby David came later. On 24 October 1939, R. J. Moulton wrote his sister, Dora Moulton Balano, about our stay at their house:

> Ouida's husband, Louis David "Bill" Coats, works for Swift & Co. They have big produce plants at Huron, S.D., Montevideo and Detroit Lakes Minn, He was transferred from Montevideo to Detroit Lakes on Sept. 10, and she expected a baby on Oct. 1.
>
> Could not locate a house or an apartment, so we had her come here to have the baby, and Bessie took care of Deanne, the little girl, while Ouida was in the hospital.
>
> The baby was born on the Oct. 1st, and Ouida came home on Oct. 11. She feels fine, says that she wants to go to a dance. And she has a nice, healthy looking boy. To go with one of the prettiest, peppiest little girls in the state.
>
> (A copy of this letter is in my files.)

---

7 "City Briefs," personals, *Evening Huronite*, 7 October 1937, p. 6, col. 4. Mrs. Moulton recovering from fall.

After Ouida and the children joined Bill, the family lived at 204 Lake Ave. N., in a house that rented for $26 per month. Bill worked 52 weeks in 1939, 60 hours in the week before the census was taken (1 April 1940), and was assistant manager of a dairy produce plant.[8]

Four generations of Sturgeses: A. E. Sturges, Bess (Sturges) Moulton with Deane in front, Ouida (Moulton) Coats, and baby David. July 1940.

8   1940 U.S. Census, Becker County, Minnesota, Detroit Lakes City, Ward 1, enumeration district 3-10, page 9B, household 200, Louis David Coates [sic]; www.ancestry.com, viewed 22 May 2013.

Coats family: Ouida, Bill, Deane, David - Dec. 1940.

Deane and David
1941

Deane and David, 1941.

LIDGERWOOD, NORTH DAKOTA
AUGUST 1940–MAY 1941

In 1940, the city of Lidgerwood had a population of 1,042. It is in Richland County, just above the South Dakota border on the east side of the state. Bill registered for the draft there on 16 October 1940. By then, he had apparently left Swift and taken a job with the Ortonville Produce Company in Lidgerwood.[9]

In 1941, Bill went to work at a poultry processing plant in St. Paul. Its owner may have been named Tilden.

ST. PAUL, MINNESOTA
MAY 1941–JUNE 1942

1257 Juliet Avenue. This was a duplex; in the other half lived a Jewish man who played Santa for us Christmas 1941. We heard "Santa's" voice, but he left before we got to see him.

Doug was born here on 2 November 1941, when typical hospitalizations for mother and child in a normal delivery was ten to fourteen days. Ouida's sister Irene had planned to come take care of David and me, but she got married instead. Ouida later commented that it cost more to pay the helper than Bill's salary for that same period of time.

All three children had chicken pox, measles, and perhaps mumps in St. Paul. I was in kindergarten and brought them home from school. Our great uncle, Dr. Chester Sturges (younger brother of Bess Moulton), who worked for the Minnesota Veterans Hospital there, made the diagnosis and put up the quarantine signs. I always heard that Doug, who had chicken pox at about six weeks of age, had only twenty-seven pox, and that David had them everywhere!

---

9 The National Archives in St. Louis, Missouri; St. Louis, Missouri; *WWII Draft Registration Cards for North Dakota, 10/16/1940-03/31/1947;* Record Group: *Records of the Selective Service System, 147;* Box: *184. Louis David Coats registration card,* serial number 2074, order number 302.

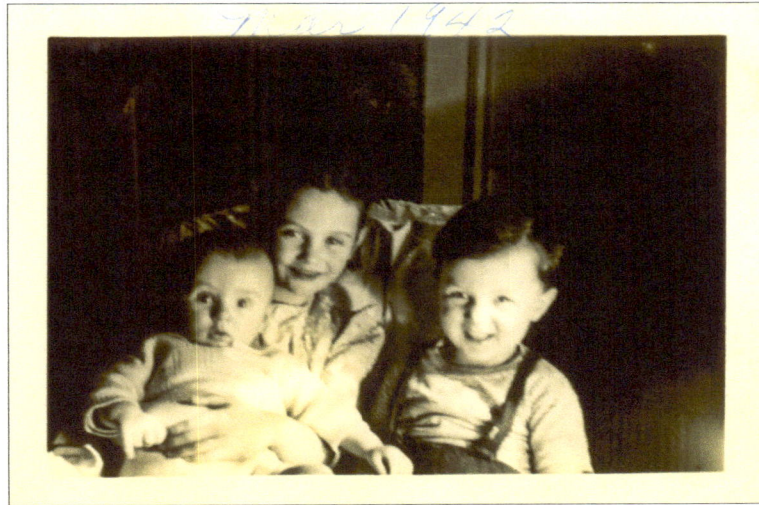

Deane holding baby Doug; next to them, brother David, March 1942.

PERRY, IOWA
JUNE 1942-SEPTEMBER 1949

The population of Perry in the 1940 census was 5,977; in the 1950 census it was 6,174. Wikipedia describes the town as "formerly a major railroad junction."

About the plant where Bill worked:

> In 1931 the Des Moines Valley Produce Co. came to Perry, moving into the old Globe Manufacturing building. For the first four years, they just bought eggs and poultry for Priebe Co. of Chicago, but in 1935 it was changed to a concentration plant.

> In October 1940 the plant was destroyed by fire. A year later, they moved into a new plant at Second and Bateman streets, and in 1945 the name was changed to Priebe and Sons, Inc.[10]

Ouida said that Bill took the job as plant superintendent with Priebe in Perry because it was common knowledge that jobs would soon be frozen for the duration of the war, and he (or they) did not want to stay in a city. The Priebe plant in Perry was right beside the railroad tracks, which ran through the middle of town. I think this was on a main route of

10 Brent Hegstrom, "Perry industries produced market winners, losers over generations," *The Perry News, We tell it all,* December 28, 2019, viewed 24 April 2020.

the Milwaukee Road that went between Chicago and points west. During the war the plant ran several shifts. We frequently went down after dinner so Bill could check on things. The children would watch the troop trains go through—I remember waving at the troops. The passenger train was called the *Hiawatha* and was supposed to be very fast.

We moved frequently during the Perry years because the folks couldn't afford to buy a house. There was a housing shortage during and right after the war, with no materials available to build new ones. They would rent a house, but when it was sold, we would have to move. Perry had three elementary (K-6) schools: Webster, Roosevelt, and Lincoln. Almost every move put us in a different school district, so we attended each of these schools at various times, some of them several times. We also spent a month or two in Pierre when I was in 4th grade, and David and I went to school there.

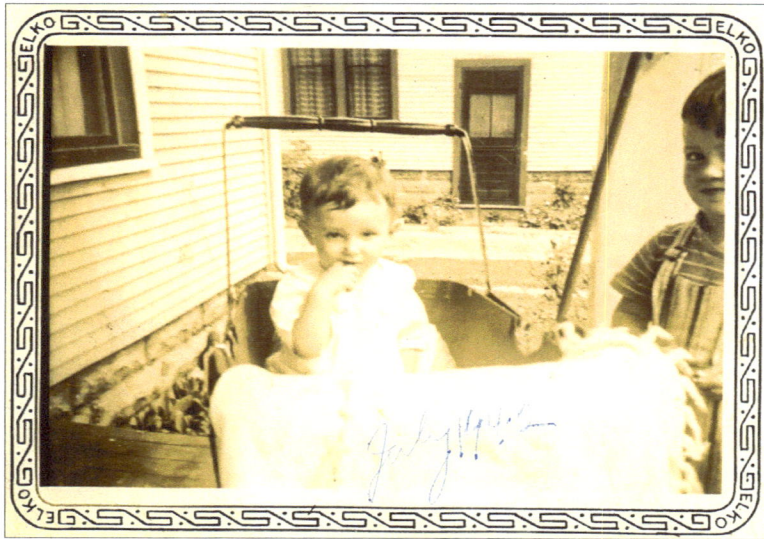

Baby Doug, with David looking on. July, 1942.

At some point we had a victory garden and at least part of the time we had to drive to it. After dinner we would all pull weeds or do other unappealing garden tasks, or so it seemed. I think no one enjoyed this, but it was considered our patriotic duty during the war, so we did it. Ouida did lots of canning during these years and perhaps some of it was produce from this garden. At some point she canned what looked like a lifetime supply of tomatoes, also peas and green beans. We didn't grow peaches; the folks bought them by the bushel, and my mother canned them, too. For many years after this I could not *stand* home-canned peaches. Ouida also canned jelly during the Perry years. Doug remembers gardens also at 708 First Street and perhaps at 1705 Evelyn.

—**2024 1st Street**, June 1942–September 1943. I don't remember whether this house had an electric refrigerator when we got there, but if there was one, at least part of the time it didn't work. Neither new refrigerators nor parts for old ones were available during the war, so we used an old-fashioned icebox that sat on the back porch. It did not keep things very cold, getting ice for it was a nuisance, and it didn't smell very good. Perhaps Bill was not very conscientious about bringing ice home—or maybe there was an ice truck that came but not often enough. An icebox certainly limited what food could be kept and for how long. Ice cream was out!

Down the street lived an older couple who were very kind to us—Edward and Mary Jordan, whom we called Grandpa and Grandma Jordan. They had a dark backyard, due to many overgrown bushes, etc. I think they babysat for us some. A small, neighborhood "mom and pop" grocery store, complete with screen door, was farther down the street (this was a double block). I would occasionally be sent to the store to get a loaf of bread or something else small. They had licorice sticks in a jar, and I got to buy some at times. Doug remembers that the sticks were two for one cent—this is all he remembers from this house.

We lived in the house during my kindergarten and (perhaps) first grade years. I skipped second grade, as the result of Ouida's triumph over Superintendent of Schools J. S. Vanderlinden. I had gone to kindergarten in St. Paul where reading was not taught at that level; Perry did teach it in kindergarten and didn't think I (or anyone) who hadn't done it there could succeed in their first grade.

Ouida probably realized it didn't matter whether I could or couldn't read, the superintendent wasn't going to let me try and stay in first grade without having gone to kindergarten there first. So I repeated kindergarten and then I went to first grade. An agreement was then reached for me to be tutored in the summer after first grade so I could enter third grade that fall. This may have been good for my education, but certainly didn't make me feel as though I fit in! The other kids at school didn't think much of this, either.

I don't remember much of what I learned in third grade, except that Abraham Lincoln freed the slaves. If the teacher said anything else about the Civil War, I have forgotten it. My only other memory from third grade is learning cursive writing, which was a big deal back then.

David and Doug were both affected by the school birthday deadline of October 1st and had to wait a year to start school. The only option to get around this was the Catholic school. Our Protestant parents would not consider this, a decision that Ouida later regretted. She felt that David had been ready for school, and that his education suffered as a result of having to wait a year. She did not feel that it hurt Doug.

—**108 Otley Ave.**, September 1943-January 1944. I draw a blank on this house.

Doug, David, and Deane.
Christmas 1943.

—**1920 W. 3rd Street**, January 1944-April 1945. The house was a big old one on a large lot with a vacant lot next to it. I think I got to have a room by myself. We lived near the Rayners. He was a banker whose his wife did not think our family was quite up to her standards. Their son Bruce was in my class and we played together some. The Meldrums, whom we called Bobbie and Mrs. Meldrum, were our back-door neighbors and introduced our family to the game of *Sorry!*. They were nice to all of us but thought the sun rose and set in David. Doug said he felt special, too. They seemed very old to me at the time, but Bobbie was still working on the railroad (he was a fireman in the 1940 census).

I had the measles here. It must have been two-week (red) measles, which can affect the eyes. Because I had eye problems, I was made to stay in bed in a darkened room for what seemed like forever. It was also at this house that David had a bad encounter with a dog and had to be rushed to the doctor for many stitches to his face and head. Doug's memory is that David got between a bitch in heat and a male dog trying to get to her. David said he "was saved by an old lady wielding a stick used to prop up clotheslines." I remember coming home to an empty house, finding bloody towels all over the place, and not knowing what was going on. The dog was quarantined to see if it had rabies, but Ouida thought it should be killed. I don't know what happened after the quarantine period, except that the dog didn't have rabies.

Doug, Deane, and David.
Christmas 1944.

Why didn't Bill serve in the military during World War II? I remember hearing, probably from Ouida, that he was exempt because he was in an essential industry. The plant was primarily processing food for the military. So it was probably true, but he would have been exempt anyway because he had young children. Late in the war Bill got a draft notice, but I have a vague memory that around the time he received it, a ceiling had been put on the draft age, and he was above it. In any case, he was almost 32 when the war broke out, so he would not have been in the first group of draftees to be called up. At one time I had the impression (but based on what I could not now say) that he was a little bit embarrassed about not having served. But Bill had three brothers and a brother-in-law who served, so the Coats family was well represented.

—2124 1st Street, April 1945-November 1945. When World War II ended in August 1945, it seemed that everyone was riding around town honking their horn, but Ouida would not honk hers. Not sure why—she was certainly glad about the end of the war! In her book, *History of Perry, Iowa*, Marjorie Patterson wrote of the war's end:

> With shouts, laughter, showers of shredded paper and wild honking of auto horns, Perry residents celebrated the end of the World War II all through the night and into the early hours of Wednesday Aug.14 and 15, 1945. The impromptu ceremony started spontaneously shortly after the news came at 6 p.m. Tuesday and gained momentum as it went along.
>
> The downtown district was soon jammed with joyous people and cars. Traffic became snarled, traffic lights could not maintain control so special police took over at the intersections.
>
> Special services at various churches were attended by local residents.[11]

—1824 Willis, November 1945-March 1946. I think this was another big old house, of which I have only a vague memory.

PIERRE, SOUTH DAKOTA
BRIEFLY

Beginning 11 March 1946 for six weeks or two months during my fourth-grade year, we had to move again because the owners of our house were selling it. When the folks could not find another house to rent in Perry, Ouida and the children went to her parents' home in Pierre until a house could be found. At least that is the explanation given then, but now I cannot help but wonder if there was more to it than that. David and I started school there the next day, another school change.

---

11 Marjorie Patterson, *History of Perry, Iowa,* vol. VIII (published by the author, ca. 1988 12 vol. typescript, [FHL #1580055]), 51-52.

It snowed on my birthday, 21 April, in Pierre. Another indelible memory is of an adult Indian man stepping off a sidewalk into the street to let me pass. I also remember that my grandmother's good friend Mrs. Hines, who lived across the street, taught me to knit. Their homes were just a block or so from the state capitol grounds that included the governor's mansion. The governor had a daughter my age and we became friends. I remember running in and out of governor's mansion—this could only happen in a state capitol located in a very small town.

Bess Moulton wrote a letter to her son Jasper and his wife ("My dear children") on 13 March 1946:

> This is a very busy household! Ouida & 3 children arrived on the bus Monday afternoon [11 March 1946] to stay until Bill can either beg, borrow or steal a place for them to live in. They hunted for a month in Perry & couldn't find anything even within a radius of 10 or 12 miles so Bill has a temporary room at a friends and Ouida & family are here. Deane & David started school— Tues A.M.—so it isn't too noisy part of the time but this is such a <u>little</u> house for so many people that our nerves are all on edge by night. However am glad we can give them a roof over their heads at least.

We may not have been the only extra people in the house then—where did they put us all! It may have been during this visit that my grandparents had a boarder named Mr. Moe. He worked for the state and had something to do with putting books into braille for the blind. I remember him showing me the braillewriter.

Perhaps this visit was when Grandpa Moulton was managing a movie theater—or maybe that was during a summer visit a little later. Doug says it was later, and he is probably right.

—708 1st Street, Perry, spring 1946-January 1949. This was a duplex and smaller than the earlier houses. There was an empty lot next door or else this house had a large lot— anyway, it was the last house before the corner. We lived on the first floor, which had the front and back doors and only two bedrooms. The other unit had an outside stairway on the driveway side of the house to the second floor; there were a variety of tenants, none of whom I remember. There was an alley behind—in fact, there might have been an alley behind all the houses in Perry. Occasionally, tramps would knock on the back door and Ouida would feed them in exchange for chores. I think she was sympathetic to their plight and looked for things for them to do so she could give them a meal.

THE CHANTICLEER

September, 1946   Published for the friends and employees of PRIEBE & SONS, INC.

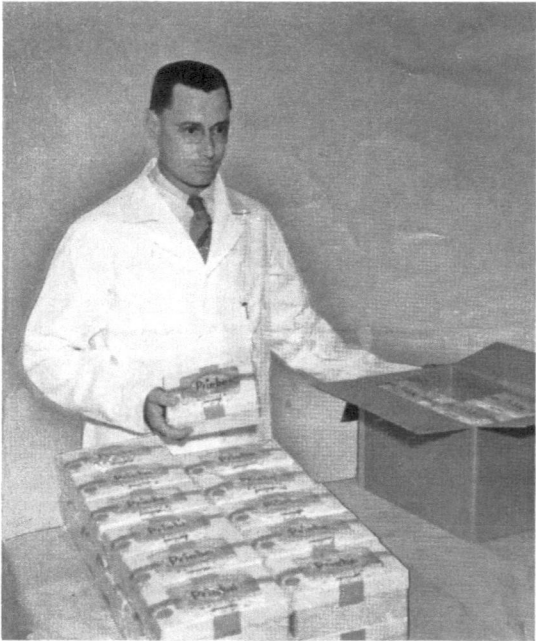

Priebe plant, Perry, Iowa, 1948.

• BILL COATS, Perry, places ready-to-cook chickens into cartons for shipment.

Ouida in front of 708 First Street, Perry, Iowa, 1947.

The basement housed a wringer washing machine (ours I think, but perhaps used by both families). All wash loads used the same wash water, then went through one or two rinse tubs and were wrung by swinging the wringer arm over to the other tubs. You started with whites and moved on down to darks, and then washed the heavy items last. Once David got his hand caught in the wringer, and when Ouida hit the release bar something flew off, hit him in the head, and he had to have stitches. Another time when she was napping, I (age ten or so) decided to do the laundry for her. I don't remember how much I got done, but I was sitting on the back steps thinking I had done something helpful. But I also woke her up in the process—and she came out the back door and kicked me in the hip. If there was any aftermath to this, I don't remember it.

The next-door neighbors here were an older couple named Myrtle and Earl (?) Cross. They were always very nice to us, but I don't think Ouida thought they quite measured up to our level! They had a grown son nicknamed "Sis" who was not working. He had been an invalid, probably due to war wounds, and did needlework to pass the time. He was also very nice to us. The senior Cross couple had a granddaughter named Shirley Cross who was a friend.

We went to Roosevelt School from this house. In my memory and Doug's, it was a long walk—Doug remembers it was twelve blocks and that seems right—and we walked home for lunch at least some of the time. The teacher I most remember was Miss Cecilia Covey, a heavy-set older woman who taught geography and probably didn't bathe as often as she might have. She liked to perch on the corner of a student desk while teaching and no one wanted her to sit on their desk! Another teacher I remember is Miss Williams, who was the grade school music teacher. From her I learned that the Lone Ranger music was from *The William Tell Overture*!

During our grade school years Ouida made candy (fudge, caramels, divinity, etc.) as gifts for our teachers at Christmas. Miss Hardy, who taught both David and Doug in first grade, is supposed to have said she was glad to get another Coats child in her class so she would get that candy at Christmas. We all considered that we had something special to give, especially the caramels.

David remembers 708 First Street being across from a milk processing plant and that there was a hybrid seed corn plant behind it. I did not remember this at all, but one of the

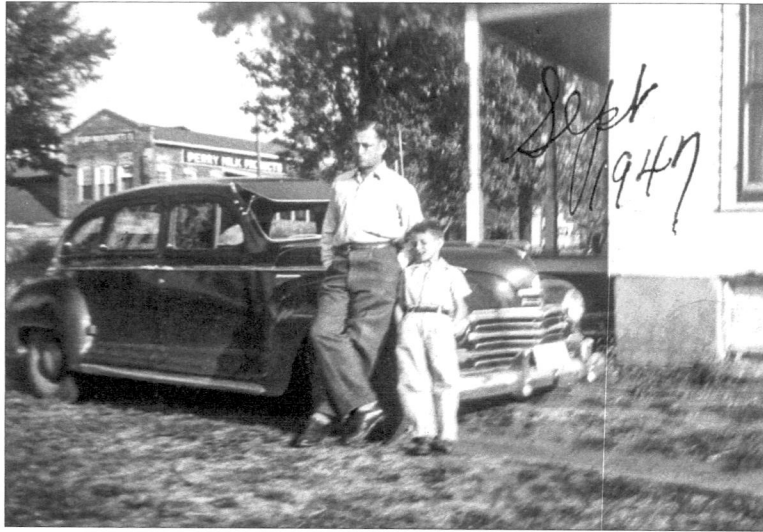

Bill and David, September 1947. Perry Milk Products in the background.

family photos taken from the side yard clearly shows the milk plant across the street.

Perry had a public swimming pool that was very popular in the summer and not too far from our house. This was in the days when the pool was drained every week, starting after closing on Sunday. The lifeguards spent Monday cleaning the pool, and it reopened on Tuesday with nice fresh water. There was chlorine in the water, but obviously the filters were not as good as those today and probably the cost of water was lower.

I remember being sent regularly to that pool during the summer. It was beyond the milk plant, and I had to ride my bike through the city park to get there. The pool was small and crowded—I have memories of it being so crowded I couldn't move. I hated going because of the sweaty ride home that left me hot and sticky. I also hated having to turn in my glasses, which were then made of glass. And you had to put your clothes in a wire basket, turn it in at the desk, and get a key that fastened to your suit. There was a footbath of some disinfectant to step in as (I think) you came out of the dressing room. At some point Ouida tried to teach me to do a standing front dive from the side of the pool. She did this by standing beside me on the deck with our raised hands together on one side and sort of falling into water headfirst. This did not go well; it was some years later before I learned to do it.

One activity I did like was sidewalk roller-skating. Our skates were the type that clamped to the sides of hard-soled shoes. You tightened the clamp with a skate key worn around the neck. All the blocks around us had sidewalks and I loved skating on them. I was not the only skater, so it was also fun socially.

David and I had our first jobs here. David remembers that in third grade he had "a small paper route (twenty something papers) on the street behind us." He also remembered "an article in the *Des Moines Tribune* calling me their youngest and smallest (the article said 3') carrier. I remember earning the money ($49) to buy a new Schwinn bike, which I got when we lived on Evelyn." The oldest he could have been at this address is nine.

I also had a paper route, for the daily Perry paper. I don't think I saved any money—there was a market, the Perry Fruit Market, that sold all kinds of candy, and I spent most of my earnings there. This was fourth or fifth grade. My other memory of the paper route is that the man at the office where we picked up the papers for delivery always called me Pants. He got a kick out of that, which made me uncomfortable. A little later, in summer after the sixth grade, I worked de-tasseling seed corn for a few weeks. That was hot work with long days in the sun. We stood on a big machine that had a number of arms, each with a small platform, and covered a number of rows of corn on each side. The machine was prone to tipping over; we were all told to hang on if that happened. It did, and I was the only one who hung on. I was unhurt and don't remember that anyone was seriously injured. I did save some money from this job and bought some clothes. It was not a job I ever wanted to do again.

Our family never took a family vacation, although Ouida and children did visit our relatives in South Dakota, usually once a year. In my memory, the parents took only one vacation by themselves. I was about 11 or 12, and I don't remember where they went or how long they were away. I do remember that the children were farmed out during that time. David spent the time with Bill's oldest brother, Leslie, and his wife on their farm near Doland. Doug stayed with Ouida's parents in Pierre. I stayed with family friends in Perry who lived in an apartment over a bar—they had a daughter about my age. I remember that we went to a carnival and I got tick in my eyelid.

In August 1948, Ouida and children went to Pierre, South Dakota, for her parents' 40th wedding anniversary. Her two siblings—sister, Irene Adermann, and brother, Jasper "Jay" Moulton—with all their children, were also there as was Marilyn Moulton (Jasper's wife) and Bess's father, A. E. Sturges.

The three Moulton siblings: Jasper standing, Irene (at left) and Ouida seated.

The August 1948 group photo of the family: back row of men, left to right, Jasper Moulton, R. J. Moulton, and A. E. Sturges; middle row, standing, left to right, Irene Adermann, Ouida with David and Doug Coats in front of her, Bess Moulton and Marilyn Moulton; front row, children seated, left to right: Fred Moulton, Beverly Adermann, three Moultons—Royal, Sandra with baby Vickie looking up at her, and Elroy Adermann—Deane Coats holding Wayne Adermann.

—**1705 Evelyn**, January-September 1949. This was a new house, the first one the folks owned, and we lived in it less than a year before moving to Estherville. The money for the purchase probably came from Bill's inheritance from his father who died in March 1948. We actually moved on or near January 1, but there must have been a tax advantage to moving before the old year ended because I remember the parents telling someone that we moved in December. I corrected them and said it was January and got firmly scolded for this later by Ouida who said something about taxes. Perhaps the tax advantage was the other way, but I was definitely scolded for correcting!

Ouida did not want to buy this house because she thought it was too small—the first floor had only two bedrooms, though there was a full basement underneath. Bill was determined to buy it, and he agreed to build a bedroom for the boys in the basement. I think he and a friend (or friends) did the work themselves. They finished the room in knotty pine and put war surplus bunk beds in it. Doug also remembers these bunk beds at 708, and that David fell out of the top bunk.

I got the second bedroom on the main floor, which was a real treat for me because all three of us children had shared a room at 708 First. I was in the seventh grade and, while recovering from the flu, I got hooked on radio soap operas. I hated to go to back to school for fear I would miss what happened next!

The house had no dining room, only a dining ell off the living room. This was where we ate, so it must have also had a small kitchen (which I cannot visualize). The folks bought a metal dinette set, the type in vogue then. One time when the folks were out, David made candy and left the dishes in the kitchen sink. He was surprised that Ouida figured out what he had done. We were only in this house till September.

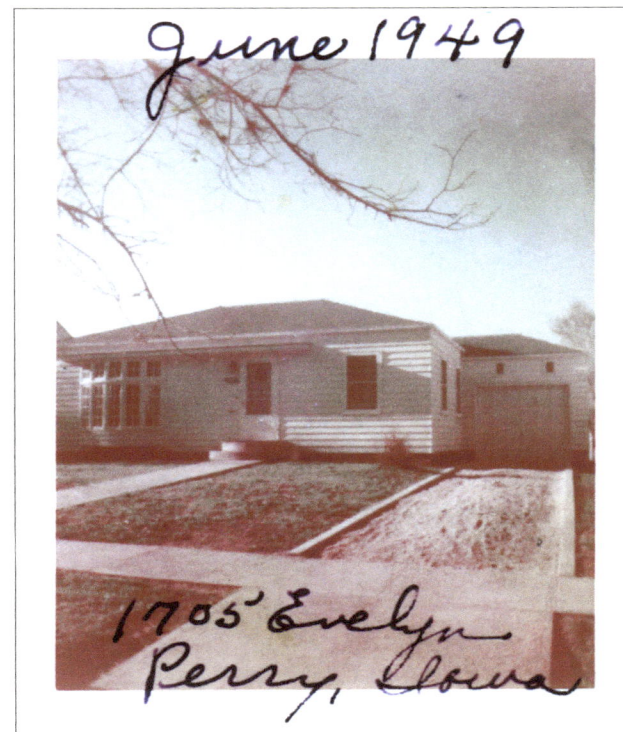

Our house on 1705 Evelyn, June 1949.

We got the piano around this time—supposedly it came out of some farm building and was not much to look at. But the sounding board was good according to the piano tuner, thus the piano lessons. I did like piano lessons much better than the dancing lessons I had taken for five or six years.

David remembers the house well and said, "[It was] real nice with a curved bay window in front. The back yard was big but fell off down hill. I remember the knotty pine bedroom in the basement. I remember Uncle Shorty [Ronald Coats] rubbing [our dog] Blackie's nose in pee to break him of doing it in the house. I remember we had a piano and Mom tried to get me to take lessons and practice, the lessons were from a Catholic nun. Needless to say they all failed. Up the street to the north was a family that had a little store. The boy my age or just older was named Dick Madrin or something like that. We used to play with them.

This house put us in Lincoln school, which was just a block south on the other side of the street. I remember not living too far (couple of blocks up and over) from Dr. Whittie, our dentist. (I remember his son becoming an Eagle Scout and then running into him (son) as a dentist in the navy.) I [also] remember listening faithfully to all the radio standards starting around 4 or 5 in the afternoon."

MORE ON OUR LIFE IN PERRY.

David said: "I have a lot of scattered memories [of Perry], but a couple that don't jive with the dates. I remember the end of WWII there at 708 1st St. I'm not sure it was V-E or V-J [Day], but I remember the family next door [*the Cross family*] with a son in the service and when the sirens etc., went off at the end of the war. I also remember when their son came home and just laid in bed reading. They had a good-sized garden and I stepped on a nail there and still have the scar. [I] also remember [being] at same address when Grampa Coats died and Dad went to the funeral. *[I also remember the scene in the kitchen of that house when Bill got the news of his father's death. DD]* [I] have plenty of memories there. Our longtime bikes. Basketball goal. Corn field. Rhubarb. Plums. Paper route with *Des Moines Tribune*. Roosevelt school. 2nd and 3rd grades."

In Perry, Ouida belonged to two bridge clubs, one auction and one contract bridge. She was also active in the Eastern Star. Bill belonged to the Masons and the Elks (B.P.O.E. for Benevolent Protective Order of Elks), but he told us it meant Best People on Earth. They went out occasionally as a couple and then we had teenage babysitters. One of our sitters was crazy about Frank Sinatra, who was all the rage then. Swooning over him was very common among teenage girls who made a big production of it. Ouida was afraid the sitter wouldn't pay any attention to us if Frank Sinatra was on the radio! This was in one of the earlier houses in Perry. By the time we lived on Evelyn, I think we no longer had babysitters.

We attended the Presbyterian Church in Perry, a red brick building that sat on a corner lot. The minister's name was Jean Pierre Hauteur, and he was pretty high on himself. Ouida was fairly active in this church. She sang in the choir, was active in the women's organization, and was president of it one year. To earn money, the ladies' group sometimes catered social functions in the church basement meeting room, and I remember being there for some of those. The older three of us were baptized there when I was ten—embarrassing to me because I was the oldest of all the ones baptized. I also remember that Bill didn't show up for it. Doug remembers getting his first Bible for reciting the 23rd Psalm. I got a white Bible for reciting that and several other standard Bible pieces (1st, 23rd, and 100th Psalms, Ten Commandments, Beatitudes, John 3:16). We also went to Bible school there for two weeks right after school closed for the year. Boring and hot!

Going to Moxley's Ice Cream Parlor was a special treat. My favorite flavor was butter brickle, something I did not see for many years after we left Perry. Bill would occasionally take us—in fact, I only remember going there when he took us.

Radio was the medium of entertainment and news in the 1940s. Early in our time in Perry, we had a floor model radio. During air raids and blackouts, when no light was supposed to show, Ouida would cover up this radio with an overcoat so she wouldn't have to miss the Bing Crosby show. By the time we lived at 708 First Street, we had a table model Philco radio record player that we children were allowed to operate. To play a record, you opened the door, slid the record in, shut the door, and it played automatically. There were Glenn Miller and Freddie Slack records in the house, but the ones I most remember were the old Victor one-sided opera recordings (with the logo of a dog listening to "His Master's Voice") that Ouida got from her mother. I listened to many of them many times, and to this day I can still recognize the sextet from the opera "Lucia di Lamermoor" by the first three notes. The singers on that one included Enrico Caruso and Ezio Pinza.

School life in the 1940s was quite different in many ways from today. In my memory none of the elementary schools in Perry I attended had clubs or offered extra-curricular activities. We never had homework, not even once that I can recall. We didn't have team sports except in physical education. I don't remember ever taking a field trip. Scout troops

The Presbyterian Church choir, April 1949. Ouida is in the front row, seventh from the left.

were independent from the school and, I think, from the churches. By about fourth grade I joined a Girl Scout troup led by Mrs. Swift. My only memory of the troop is of her husband playing the musical saw for us. I don't think there were Brownie or Cub Scout troops in Perry then. David talks about liking Boy Scouts later on, in Concord.

Ouida did her grocery shopping at the A&P supermarket on Saturday afternoons, and when we were too young to leave alone, she had to take all of us with her. That was the only time she would have access to the car. In the summer, we had our main meal at noon so Bill could go straight from work to the golf course to play golf. He also played softball and coached a team for a while. He bowled in the winter at a bowling alley that was upstairs. I remember trying to bowl there, too, but I made awful scores!

There was a red popcorn stand on the main corner downtown run by a farmwoman who always wore a white uniform at the stand. It was only open on Saturdays, when all the farmers came to town, and I remember it as having the world's best popcorn. She always said something to the effect that for good grub, you salt it before [or after?] you cook it. David remembers, "She made white popcorn (still my favorite), and sold it in bags up to grocery size. You could also buy a bag of 'old maids' for very little on special occasions."

The public library in Perry was a big old Carnegie library building with a long flight of stairs up to the front door, probably standard Carnegie architecture. In an old photo, it doesn't seem so large now. Ouida was a frequent patron there, as she was everywhere we lived. When I was about in third grade she took me to the children's room and showed me a shelf with a series of animal stories that I just loved—I can still see that shelf. Probably the stories were by Thornton Burgess or Ernest Thompson Seton.

Another book that made a big impression on me was *Snow Treasure* by Marie McSwigan. It's about children in Norway who helped move their country's gold reserves to safety by sledding across the border into Sweden with the gold fastened under their sleds. I must have read it soon after it came out in 1943. By the time I went to work at the library in Falls Church, Virginia, many years later, I remembered the story but not the title. It was like finding an old friend when I ran across it in the 1970s.

It was probably in the Perry library that I first read two books that I looked for in the library of every town we moved to after that. Today we would probably describe them as YA or young adult titles. One was *Christina*, about a very unhappy teenage girl whose serious overweight problem was only part of her misery; she also lived with a family who didn't like or want her and was a farm drudge. Finally, she ran away to the circus and became the fat lady. But because she was happy there, after a while she had to wear padding in her costumes to fill them up. Eventually she found true happiness and, if I remember rightly, romance as well.

The other was titled *Karen*, about a Scandinavian immigrant girl who worked on a farm, got married, and pulled on a rope tied to the foot of the bed during the labor and delivery of her first child. There must have been lots of other hardships in the story but the rope is the main thing I remember.

During the war, women's stockings were in very short supply. This was about the time silk stockings were being replaced by nylon, then considered inferior to silk. Stockings had a seam up the back of the leg. When women couldn't get stockings, they sometimes resorted to a cosmetic pencil to draw the line up the back of their legs so it looked like they had them on. Cigarettes were also scarce, and Ouida rolled some of her own with a little machine that had a hand crank that turned out very wobbly looking cigarettes. Other wartime memories are of ration books and stamps for food, shoes, and clothing; saving grease, fat, and tin foil; buying savings bonds in stamp books at school. It also seemed that we ate chicken all the time, and I grew to dislike it heartily. Now I eat it frequently.

Several times during the war, Ouida and all of us children went by train to Pierre to visit her folks. Trains were very crowded then, with extra seats that folded down across the aisle. I remember always getting gum in my hair on these trips and having to have it cut out.

Another memory of Perry is going to the movies. There were two theaters, the Perry and the Dallas, both on the same block—I am no longer sure which one was which. One showed so-called A movies, the big-name ones, and I went there every Sunday. The other theater showed B movies, mostly cowboy movies that always included an adventure serial with cliff-hanger endings. I went there every Saturday. My favorite cowboy movies were those with Gene Autry and the ones about the Durango Kid, played by Charles Starrett. The A movie theater had lots of musicals and family features such as stories featuring Lassie or other animals. Admission for a child was ten cents at each theater. My twenty-five cent allowance got me into both—one on each weekend day. On Sunday, I spent the extra nickel at the snack bar. I liked popcorn, but I probably bought Milk Duds more often.

Mostly, we were all healthy during the Perry years. We were among the few children who didn't have tonsillectomies—I remember feeling deprived about this, not getting to stay home and have ice cream—because Ouida could see no reason for it when we were healthy. There were several polio scares when we lived in Perry, and we even knew a child who got bulbar polio and was in an iron lung for a while. Her name was Mary Ann Burland; fortunately she recovered completely. But it was a scary time—swimming pools were closed, and people were advised to keep their children away from crowds.

Ouida had very poor teeth. When we lived in Perry, fluoride treatments for teeth became available and we all had them. She didn't want us to have teeth like hers. Bill had wonderful teeth.

About my sixth-grade year, I remember a *big* scandal about a Dr. Elvidge who lost his medical license for performing abortions. He may have been our doctor. At any rate, Ouida had some sympathy for him.

In spring 1949, we learned we were soon to have a new sibling. Both David and I remember that the folks made picking a name for the new baby a family affair and had a meeting where we voted on names. Because the rest of us had names starting with D, the new baby's name also had to start with D. I think we picked Donald for a boy. Ouida wanted Deborah for a girl, but we outvoted her and picked the name Donna. Ouida was later glad because at the time many little girls were being named Deborah.

Why did we leave Perry? David remembers that Bill was "plant superintendent at Priebe's and Joe Kidd was the manager." David also said, "Bill liked Joe okay, but Joe took advantage of him and jerked him around some." (*I have no trouble believing that—I remember him as a slimy type—a perfect slick salesman. DD*) David added, "Once Bill had bought the house, Joe thought he had him. Joe did something that made Bill so mad he quit, house or no house, and took a job with Paul Gray in Estherville. Several years later, Frank Priebe (whom Bill liked) asked him to come back to Priebe and work in Concord under Joe Kidd. Bill had an excellent reputation in the business, and Joe got the benefit of it. He turned out such a good product that people were willing to pay more for it—this was in the days when inspection wasn't as strict as it later became." Reputation must have mattered more before stricter inspection.

Doug remembers the same story about why we left. He also remembers that Ouida later told him that people had made anonymous phone calls in Perry linking Bill with Martha McDevitt who worked at the plant.

More on people mentioned above:

- **Joe and Harriet Kidd and their two children, Bobby and Dolores.** Joe—manager of Priebe and Dad's boss—and his family lived in a big house not far from an elementary school. In today's terms, they would no doubt be considered an extremely dysfunctional family. The parents drank too much, and Bobby was spoiled and bad news. Doug remembers that he and David got into Ex-Lax gum at their house and paid the price. I remember Bobby telling a story about putting urine in a glass and telling Dolores it was juice and she drank it. He went at some point to a military boarding school (Culver Military Academy in Indiana?). We thought that being sent to that kind of school was an indication that you were a problem child. It was very different from North Carolina, where boarding school, military and otherwise, was not uncommon among families who could afford it. Later, Joe Kidd and family moved to North Carolina about the same time we did. He was manager of the Concord plant when Bill was plant superintendent there. The Kidds lived in Charlotte.

- **Martha and LeVere McDevitt**. Martha worked at the Perry plant, in the back end. She wore a white uniform and was probably a supervisor. LeVere, a butcher, was a good-natured Irishman who probably had a drinking problem. He was in the Navy during World War II and Martha is supposed to have said if he survived she would join the Catholic Church, which she had previously refused to do. He did and she did. They had no children, were good to us kids, and on friendly terms with both parents despite rumors about Bill and Martha. One family story has it that the two couples rustled a cow during the war, and then Bill and LeVere butchered it. But they were afraid of getting caught, so the meat was not used. David heard another version of the story in which they bought the cow in Jamaica, Iowa, butchered it in a barn there, but again were afraid to use the meat for the same reason. Ouida appeared to like Martha and consider her a good friend. She kept up with them for quite a few years after we moved away.

ESTHERVILLE, IOWA
SEPTEMBER 1949-MARCH 1951.

Donna was born here 30 September 1949, and Estherville became one of the two towns we lived in before moving to Concord.

Ouida was pregnant with Donna, near term, and determined to move before the baby was born. Her theory was that the baby was easier to move in the tummy than after its birth. We moved a few weeks after school started in Perry; I was in the eighth grade. Bill had gone on ahead, though I don't recall how much ahead. Again, he could not find a house for us. In addition to the poultry plant, his boss, Paul Gray, owned a summerhouse on Lake Okoboji. We moved there temporarily so the family could leave Perry. The children went to school by bus to Spirit Lake. On September 29th, Ouida started in labor during the day and waited till we got home from school to drive to Estherville. Bill came on the run when I went into the plant and told him what the situation was! Donna was born after midnight that day, on September 30th, about a week after we moved there.

After the brief stay at Lake Okoboji we moved to 420 North 6th in Estherville and went to school there—our third school system that year, and all before Thanksgiving.

—**420 N. 6th**, October 1949 to about the beginning of summer 1950. Bill and Ouida bought this house and within the year, according to the mother of a school friend, they lost it. She said she saw it in the newspaper—I was mortified when she told me. Neither of my parents ever mentioned that in my hearing.

An older house, 420 was about a block from the school. The previous owners had not been good housekeepers, to say the least. The kitchen walls were filthy, and I remember Bill painting the walls yellow. He also painted the bathroom on the first floor (I can't remember if there was another one upstairs) where some previous female had deposited her used sanitary napkins behind the bathtub, an old-fashioned one with legs. Ouida was aghast over this; I expect Bill was, too, but he never said anything about it in my hearing. There were at least three bedrooms upstairs; mine connected to the parents' room through my closet.

I was in my movie star phase that year, buying every movie fan magazine known to man, and virtually papering the wall in my room with the full-page color photos often included in the magazines. Ouida did not give me a hard time about this for some reason, and I never did it again in any other house. This was also the year I thought cowboy and western singer Eddie Arnold was just wonderful. I especially loved his recording of "The Cattle Call." A friend who owned the recording used to call me and play it over phone. It featured lots of yodeling.

Donna was an infant when we lived here and, of course, was in diapers. Ouida had to wash diapers no matter what the weather was. Like most folks then, we didn't have an automatic clothes dryer. In the winter she had to hang diapers outside where they frequently froze on the line, were stiff as a board when brought in, and damp when defrosted.

This was about the time that the card game Canasta became a craze that swept the county. Everybody was playing it and we did, too. We had some neighbors who were avid players, and we played at every opportunity. I think all of us except Donna did play—I know I did. After a few years its popularity waned in the United States.

After 420 N. 6th was sold, we rented a house at Spirit Lake for the summer of 1950. I remember that Bill's brother Shorty (Ronald Coats) and his bride, Marylee, visited us on their honeymoon and were embarrassingly (or so I considered it then) lovey-dovey. Shorty gave me tips on some furniture I was refinishing.

During that summer, I witnessed an unsuccessful attempt to save a drowning victim. A couple on their honeymoon capsized their boat not far from our house, and rescuers brought them ashore near us. The woman was laid out on the ground where they worked on her for some time. When artificial respiration didn't work, they used a huge needle to put a yellow fluid into her chest to try to restart her heart. They saved her husband but couldn't revive her. I have never forgotten that sight.

The Coats family: back row, left to right, Bill holding Donna, Deane, and Ouida; front row, left to right: David and Doug. July 1950.

—**714 N. 6th**, fall 1950 to late winter or early spring 1951. This house was a rental, on the same street as the other house, a few blocks farther from downtown and the school. It was not as large or nice as the first. The upstairs was *very* cold, but I have no mental picture of the layout there. In my memory, the house was long and rather narrow with a first-floor bedroom the folks used. I remember having lots of fights with Bill that year, which Ouida said or implied were entirely my fault. I accepted this for many years. Once, a few years later, I asked her why they didn't give me away. Her answer was "Who would have had you?"

There was a coal furnace in the basement and a big floor vent (several feet square in a grid pattern) in the first floor hall just outside the kitchen. This was the main and probably the only source of heat for that area, and it did get *hot* when the furnace was running. I don't remember whether there were additional vents on that floor, but the heat for the upstairs was solely from the hot air rising from that vent, up through a grate in the first-floor ceiling/second-story floor.

That first-floor vent caused the burn on Donna's lower leg that resulted in a crisscross scar. Late one afternoon when Ouida was fixing dinner, she heard Donna cry briefly then stop, so she didn't investigate. When she was undressing Donna for bed, she discovered the burn and always felt terrible that she hadn't realized what happened at the time. Her theory was that Donna had fallen with her pant leg up, but it came back down when she stood up, and that's why it wasn't noticed. Donna still has that scar but it has lightened over time.

Miss Henrietta Miller, whom students called Hank behind her back, was principal of the junior high. An old maid teacher who seemed ancient to me then, she ran a fairly tight ship and could be quite stern. She was quite tall, had a hook nose (sort of), and gray hair in a bun. She taught Palmer Method penmanship to eighth graders and made an indelible impression on me. Everyone in the class had to complete a form set known as a business form. My one great accomplishment in that class was learning to make a (nearly) perfect Z! The form was a lot of work, and Hank insisted that it be done properly. Perhaps we had to use pens, pen points, and dip ink—this was before widespread use of ballpoint pens and I don't recall whether we could use fountain pens.

My other memory of Hank concerns an incident in which another student threw up in class. Unfortunately, some of the vomitus landed on my books that were on the floor next to my desk. Hank took them away, had them cleaned, and then brought them back to me. I then made the mistake of picking them up and smelling them! What exactly she did at that point I don't recall, but I do remember it conveyed to me her very great disapproval of this action!

The public school system there included a two-year college, Estherville Junior College, with a very popular basketball team. Everybody went to their games and yelled for the EJC Wolves to "fight, fight, fight." I remember the saying on the wall that went something like this: "And when the one great scorer comes to write against your name, he marks not that you've won or lost, but how you played the game."

Some years later, David and his wife, Kathy, had friends from Estherville and were able to go over memories with them. David remembers the first lake house: "We were living there when Donna was born (my 10th b'day). Still have my birthday present from then, a leather zipper notebook that Dad paid $5 for. I also remember the folks forgetting my birthday until Mom remembered it in the hospital the night of the 1st, and Dad took me downtown to the drug store (still there), and I picked out the zipper notebook. I also remember we were all supposed to go to school the day Donna came home but you [DD] faked us out by walking out to the bus with us and then backing out when we were already on. [*Guilty as charged. DD*] This was all at the Lake O house. Remember one house across from the school in E'ville and one farther down the street away from town (where Donna fell on the heater grate and scarred her leg). With the help of friends from there, I could have a long talk about that. I have hazy thoughts where Spirit Lake fits in but have strong memories of it. Also, I remember meeting L. I. Wilder or her sister who lived there." [*I think it may have been her daughter, Rose Wilder Lane, who lived somewhere in the vicinity. DD*]

CHEROKEE, IOWA
MARCH–AUGUST 1951

We lived in a new house with a muddy yard. I only remember one house, but I have two addresses so we must have lived in two different houses there.

—**117 4th S.W.**

—**125 South 7th Street**.

David's notes on Cherokee: "I mostly remember hating it. I almost got shot there (long story). Do remember the new house. Still had Blackie. Strong memories of radio programs and family gathering to listen. Hilly town and area. Remember playing war games outside of town." *[I remember that Blackie scratched his back on Donna's crib by standing up under it. He was part Cocker and the other part was large. DD]*

We got some really good photos of our baby sister during this period.

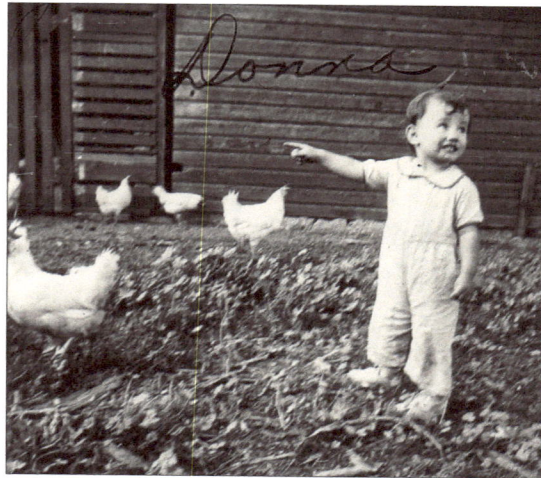

Donna Coats, May 1951. [I really love this photo, but perhaps Donna doesn't like it as much. DD]

Donna and chickens, June 1951. [We were obviously at a farm but not now sure whose it was. DD]

15 June 1951, all four children, back row: David and Doug (who looks unhappy); front row: Deane and baby Donna.

Life in Cherokee was not a happy time in my memory! We came in two-thirds of the way through the school year and didn't fit in. Soon after we moved there, Bill took a job with Priebe & Sons in Concord, N.C., and by May 1951, he had gone on. Ouida and all four children stayed in Cherokee until around the first of August. I am not sure why we didn't move right after school was out, but perhaps Bill couldn't find a suitable house before then.

The drive down had taken four days. Ouida had to do all the driving as none of us was old enough to have a drivers' license. She had the two boys in the front seat with her; I was in the back seat with Donna (age 22 months), and my job was to keep her happy. Ouida bought disposable diapers for Donna, then a fairly new product and much different from today's disposables. My strongest memory of the trip is being required to throw the dirty diapers out the window. Ouida said Donna had been ready to be trained for some time—she would lie down on the floor and put her legs in the air when she wanted a clean diaper—but Ouida had decided it would have to wait until after the move.

CONCORD, NORTH CAROLINA
AUGUST 1951–JULY 1956

Deane graduated from high school here.

"J. M. Kidd Comes to Concord to Manage Poultry Plant," the *Concord Tribune* reported on 24 May 1951.[12] There were several paragraphs about Joe and his family, then this information about what the plant did and a brief mention of Bill:

> The Priebe and Sons Company which has acquired a long lease on the Poultry Processing plant here, operates 14 poultry and egg processing plants in the middle west, but this is its first venture into the south. Most of its plants are in Iowa, Illinois, Kansas, Missouri, and South Dakota, and are well known in those states. The Priebe and Sons Company, in which Mr. Kidd is a director, has been in business 60 years. In addition to all its 14 plants, the company maintains a New York Sales Branch through which is marketed dressed, drawn, and frozen poultry products, shell eggs, and dried eggs.

---

12 "J. M. Kidd Comes to Concord to Manage Poultry Plant," *Concord Times*, 24 May 1951, sect. 2, p. 4, c. 1.

The greater portion of the output of the Concord plant, Mr. Kidd said, is now going to the U.S. Government for the use of the armed forces. It buys most of its living poultry for processing within a radius of from 15 to 25 miles of Concord. Coming to Concord with Mr. Kidd is his plant superintendent, Louis J. Coats, also from Perry, Iowa. He, too is planning to move to Concord as soon as he can find a suitable home for himself, his wife and their four children.

A 1955 article tells more about the scope of work the plant did:

At the Concord plant, Priebe & Sons handles annually around 3,500,000 broilers and fryers, amounting to approximately 10,000,000 lbs. of birds. Live chickens are purchased from growers in Cabarrus, Chatham, Union, Wilkes and other counties up to 100 miles away. Each year chicken growers are paid about $2,500,000 for chickens processed in the plant. The firm operates eight large live poultry trucks in picking up chickens at the farms. These chickens are all completely eviscerated, ready for the cooking pan. All are government inspected and they are shipped over the entire United States. Probably half of the plant's production is purchased by the Federal Government and shipped to government installations for the armed forces in this and numbers of foreign countries. Gross annual sales reach approximately $4,000,000. Joseph M. Kidd is plant manager; L. D. Coats is plant superintendent, and Alan Graves is office manager. Mr. Kidd and Mr. Coats came to Concord in 1951 to take over the plant and install needed equipment and machinery.[13]

13 *E. S. C. Quarterly*, vol. 13, no. 1- 2 (Winter Spring 1955), Employment Security Commission of North Carolina. Viewed 22 November 2020, https://digital.ncdcr.gov/digital/collection/p249901coll22/id/451981.

Ouida and children arrived in Concord in early August and stayed at the Colonial Motel (not far from the plant) for several days until the furniture arrived.

—**112 South Spring Street**. When Doug, Donna, and I visited Concord about 1992 or 1993, the houses had been renumbered and our house on South Spring Street, though still standing, was no longer 112. We had a hard time finding it. For one thing it looked so much smaller than we remembered it! We drove up and down the street several times and finally could only be sure which one it was by its proximity to the post office and the Lutheran Church.

My memory is of a big old house (squat and appears much smaller from the street) that was set fairly close to the street on a lot that sloped so sharply downward towards the back that you could walk out to the back yard from the basement. The basement was large, with a dirt floor, a latticework wall on the rear, and an old coal furnace with a stoker. I was happy that my brothers had to shovel coal and I didn't! There was an old washing machine that sat up on a concrete block.

112 South Spring Street, Concord, N.C. Coats home 1951-1956.

The first floor had a porch, center hall, four fairly good-sized rooms (two on each side of the hall), plus a kitchen, horrible bathroom, and a screened back porch. On the right were the living room, dining room, kitchen; on the left, a room that housed our first TV, the parents' bedroom (with a small bed for Donna), and that poor excuse for a bathroom. It was the only bathroom in the house, long and narrow, with antique plumbing. There was no shower, and it took a long time to get even a couple inches of water into the bathtub— twenty minutes is the number I remember, but perhaps it only seemed that long. As I recall, a lot less bathing went on than was ideal (at least on my part)! It just took too long to get enough water, there wasn't much hot water, and there were too many of us. Our collective memories are cloudy on the question of where the piano was, but probably it was in the dining room so as not to disturb TV-watchers.

The second floor had three bedrooms and a big sunporch-type of room across the back. My bedroom was at the front and had three windows facing the street—I think I got first choice and picked this one, though I don't think it was the largest room. I must have liked the windows, though I could have had no idea of how visible I would be if the shades weren't drawn. No one ever said anything, but when I think about it now I suppose anyone looking in got a pretty good view! I kept some of my clothes dispersed all over the floor. When Ouida had a cleaning lady, she was instructed to pick up our clothes, dust under them, and put them back down on the floor. We were supposed to pick up after ourselves!

Deane Coats — 112 South Spring Street, Concord. Nov. 1951.

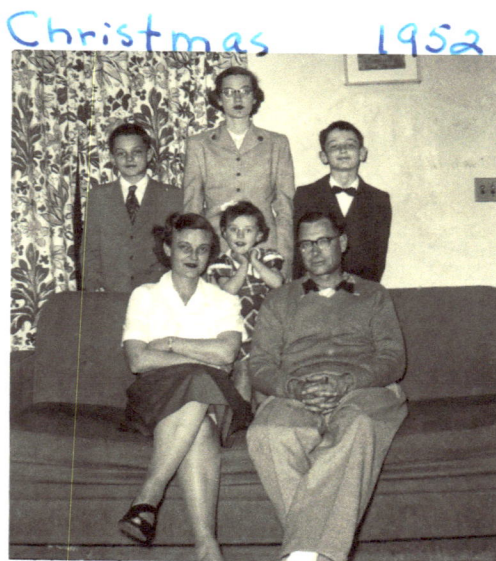

Christmas 1952

The Coats family.

1953

On her 40th Birthday!

Ouida Coats.

Doug, 1955.

David, 1955.

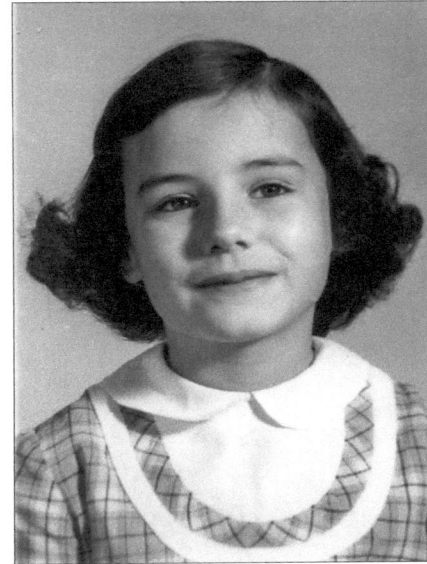

Donna, 1956.

Deane & Donna Coats,
7 April 1956. Concord, N.C.

Straight down the hallway to the back were two more bedrooms, one on either side, David's on the right and Doug's on the left. The big porch at the back had windows at least across the back and perhaps on three sides. It wasn't heated and was miserably cold in the winter and miserably hot in the summer, so it wasn't used much. Once or twice Ouida tried to make a room for Donna there, but it just wasn't comfortable enough. Donna moved into my room the day I left for college; she was in nursery school that year. Ouida trained her to walk the four or five blocks to school and back home by herself. Ouida thought it was rather amusing the Donna was known as the child who walked.

Nothing much had been done to modernize or keep the house up. It was large and located conveniently near the center of town, but rather dark and not cheerful at all. It badly needed painting inside and I remember one summer Ouida had us paint the first floor hall, which was especially dirty. Rather than buy paint to go all the way up the stairs, she drew a line even with the first floor ceiling on the wall going up the stairs and that's how far we painted. Even then I thought that line looked a bit strange! After that I think she got the landlord to paint a couple of the first-floor rooms. The bedrooms may have been wallpapered. There were four fireplaces on the first floor, at least two of which were back to back at an angle, with a shared chimney. We used the back screened porch a lot on summer evenings. Both parents, but especially Ouida, liked to sit there.

There was a pecan tree in the back yard, a new kind of tree to us transplanted Yankees. The first year we were there, Ouida had us shell pecans for gifts for relatives in the Midwest. Mostly, she didn't have much luck getting them shelled all at once, but had more success telling us she would make cookies or other goody if someone would shell nuts. The pecans were great, but the outer covering was nasty and the shells were hard!

Ouida was a coffee drinker throughout our childhoods—it seemed that she always had a cup of it handy. She must not have thought it was good for children because she didn't let us have any. She was also a smoker, but I remember her saying that cigarettes were coffin nails, and also that every cigarette shortened one's life by x (twenty?) minutes. She had favorite proverbs/maxims/idioms and used them often. I remember her definition of housework: "First you dig a hole, then you fill it up, then you dig a hole, etc." Other favorites included "put things away as you go" (when cooking, especially when baking); "if a little bit is good, a lot is better"; "Let's not [do something] and say we did" when she didn't want to go or do [something]; and "everybody eats a peck of dirt during their life." Donna remembered: "Ugly as homemade sin"; "Something [looks like something] the cat dragged in"; "Housework isn't a moral issue"; and "X is rude, crude, and socially unacceptable." Doug remembers that if he said something isn't fair, her response was: "No it's not and nobody ever said it had to be. And it's not!"

In early October 1952, Bess Moulton asked her children to come to Pierre as their father, R. J. Moulton, was seriously ill. For financial and distance reasons, the whole Coats family could not go. Ouida's brother Jasper, who lived in Montreal, decided to drive in hopes of being able to take their father for car rides, which he really enjoyed. Ouida and Donna took the bus to Harrisburg, Pennsylvania, to meet Jasper and his daughter Sandra. But by the time they got to Pierre, they were too late. Their father had died on 5 October, shortly before their arrival. They and Ouida and Jasper's sister Irene Adermann were there for the funeral and final arrangements.

Ouida and Donna detoured via Montreal on their way home. On the trip, Donna wore a checked coat that Ouida had struggled to make. Sewing was difficult for Ouida because she had a benign essential tremor and her hands shook all the time. If she walked across the room with a cup and saucer, they clattered. She could do most things with her hands well enough, but she didn't often undertake sewing projects. She saved hand sewing for her mother when she visited; Ouida also saw to it that I learned how to sew.

David's notes on Concord: The house number is now 116 or 118. When he visited Rodney (more on Rodney later), David was "crushed to find out that Union Street was not the wide grand avenue I remembered," but it still had all of

Donna in Beaconsfield, Montreal, wearing the checked coat that Ouida made. Photo taken by Jasper's family.

the trees left over from Hurricane Hazel (1954) when many had been blown down. David's only really good memories from there are from the Boy Scouts. "I had a hard time but finally found Camp Cabarrus where I had spent much time. My overall aura of Concord is not good," he said.

I agree completely with David that Concord was not a good place for our family. It had the typical southern town social structure, with people at the top and on the bottom, but not so much place for people in the middle, or at least we didn't find them. Having family connections was critical; we didn't have any there and were not rich. We were Yankees at a time when that still caused comment. Generally we didn't fit in, or at least I didn't. It wasn't till I got to college and made congenial friends that I began to think I might not be a complete misfit. I later thought Ouida's choice to go to the First Presbyterian Church was a mistake. That is where the upper crust went. There was another Presbyterian church that might have been a much better fit for us. Hindsight.

During the second semester of my first year of college, 1954-1955, I received a notice that my tuition had not been paid for that semester and if not paid by a certain date, I would have to leave. It referred me to the student aid office if I needed help. This was a big shock because I believed that it had been paid. The director of the student aid office approved me for a loan—and told me to make sure that my father, not me, was the one to pay it back. Apparently he did. If there were any parental discussions with me on this, I have blotted them out, but I don't think there were.

It is impossible to know how much impact Concord as a place may have had on the parents' marriage or whether there were problems earlier when we were too young to notice. But in Concord it was clear to me and probably David and Doug as well that, for whatever reason, they were having great difficulties. We don't know how or if they communicated about problems. According to Ouida, her parents had bickered a lot and she did not want to live that way. Bill was gambling and lost the car for nonpayment. Ouida was upset and worried about their marriage. Once, when I was in high school, I asked her why she didn't leave him. She said she couldn't leave—what would she do? And I think she worried about appearances perhaps because she had grown up where her parents—the superintendent of schools and an eighth grade teacher—were big fish in a little pond. The tension shows in this 1952 photo of the "happy couple."

Bill was arrested for drunk driving for which his driver's license was later revoked for a year. Ouida was mortified by the notice in the local newspaper: "Coats Facing Police Charge."[14] It was a short article, 1-5/8 inches high, with fairly good-sized print in the heading. I checked the week of November 14 and did not find any further report. Ouida was mortified by this and commented to one of us that they didn't have to make the print so big. The article read:

> A charge of drunken driving today had been lodged against Lewis Coats, 44, of 112 S. Spring St. City police said Coats was arrested at 8:40 p.m. yesterday on Odell St. He posted $200 appearance bond for Cabarrus Recorder's Court trial Nov. 14.

That turned out to be only the beginning of big drama that would unfold in later years. I will include it here, as it was happening simultaneously, though we children had no way of knowing until decades later.

Around the same time of Bill's drunk driving arrest, he became involved with Dorothy (Goforth) Edwards, who also worked at Priebe & Sons. This resulted in two sons, Rodney and Dennis Edwards, born in 1956 and 1957 and unknown to Bill's other children until November 1998 when Dennis contacted me, as I was the first listed child in Bill's obituary. Dennis included photos of himself and his mother. I thought Dennis resembled David and that his mother looked like Ouida did when she was younger. Subsequent DNA testing on them and Bill's four known children confirmed that, yes, he was their father. We have no evidence that Bill ever publicly acknowledged them or assisted their mother in any way. By the time we learned about this, anyone who could give us firsthand information had already died. Doug called anyone else we could think of who might have known about it, without success. (We invited Rodney and Dennis to our sibling

Ouida and Bill Coats, mid-1950s, 112 South Spring Street.

14 *Concord Tribune*, (Concord, N.C.), 27 Oct 1955, 4B.

reunion in 1999, which seemed to go well. After that, David kept in touch with them, and Donna was Facebook friends with Rodney. Perhaps we might have had more contact if any of us had lived near them.)

Notes on my telephone conversation with Doris (Jolly) Wilborn (Bill's wife after Ouida died) on 3 May 1998: Doris didn't know about that relationship but suggested that it could have developed out of Bill's efforts to help a young woman on her own with several children. Doris said that when she worked on the line at the Hiddenite plant, she had been having a hard time financially (divorced with four children). Bill had her supervisor offer her a better job (in the office, having to do at least partly with personnel). She felt that he knew she was having a hard time and tried to help, and she was grateful for the opportunity. She also volunteered the information that he never tried to date her at that time. But my brothers both think Bill was having an affair with Doris prior to her marriage to Franklin Wilborn.

Notes from another conversation with Doris, December 24, 2000: She said Franklin Wilborn first worked for Bill in Roxboro, Franklin's hometown. Sometime after Bill went to Hiddenite, Franklin and a group from the Roxboro plant came down to see the operation. Not long after that, Franklin began working for Bill in Hiddenite. That was where he met Doris.

At some point Franklin mentioned to Doris that Bill had a girlfriend who had died. Doris thought that might have been in the late 1960s, but isn't sure (or didn't want to say). When Bill was in Lumberton (I think that was probably when Donna was a senior in high school and she and Ouida were in Statesville), Bill asked Franklin to come to work there. He and Doris had a house trailer, which they moved there. On the way to Lumberton, Bill offered Doris a ride in his car rather than her having to ride in the truck or whatever was pulling the trailer. Franklin told her no—she was not riding with Bill! The time frame, per Doris's memory is between her working at the Hiddenite Grill and going to the restaurant she later worked in for some years (Scotty's??).

It wasn't clear from the conversation whether Franklin thought Bill had one or multiple girlfriends, but I suspect the latter. Doris was very diplomatic! I did tell her that I had heard he had girlfriends but that I did not have any details. I also wonder now whether the girlfriend who died, perhaps in the late 1960s, may have been Dorothy Edwards, mother of

Dennis and Rodney, who died 28 February 1974 in Concord. And what, if anything, would that mean? Or was there another girlfriend who died?

∽

From here on most comments are by David, Doug, and Donna. From fall 1954 and going forward, I was in college or working or married and never really lived at home again except on college breaks.

SOUTHERN PINES, NORTH CAROLINA
JULY 1956-JULY 1958

David graduated from high school here.

—**Carthage Road,** 1 August 1956–1 October 1957. Donna remembers this house as "one story and a few miles out in the country." She said, "I remember that there was a field and forest behind the house, and I remember picking huckleberries there with neighborhood kids and having mother make huckleberry pie. It was a small brick house." Donna was in second that grade year.

—**145 May Street**; Fall 1957–July 1958. Donna described the second house in town as "a two-story brick house very close to the school and only a couple of blocks from the main street and from the Schweigers." She said, "I got a Barbie doll at that house; it was the first year they were produced. My Barbie doll was stolen and I never got another one. I also remember skating in Southern Pines with those skates that attached to the bottom of shoes." The family lived there "for my some or all of my third-grade year. We have those Easter pictures taken in front of the first house, and we have

Coats family photo, 21 April 1957.

51

pictures of me in a dancing costume and David in a cap and gown at the house in town. Mostly, I remember the Schweigers and spending lots of time with them. I also remember going to the movies every Saturday afternoon in town." *[Vince & Marge Schweiger and their two daughters were good family friends. Vince was a veterinarian and the USDA inspector at the plant. DD]*

David remembers: "145 May St. was US 1 and right next to the school. Oxford Road went to Carthage (county seat), I think. It was out past a couple of golf courses and a hospital. Arthur Godfrey had a manor a few miles past it towards Carthage. Again, not a lot of good memories. As in Concord I was an outsider and had only a few good friends."

Deane: I have only two memories from Southern Pines. The first is coming "home" from summer school shortly after the move in 1956 and not knowing where "home" was. I had to call for someone come get me! The second is finding an old copy of Jane Austen's *Pride and Prejudice* upstairs in one of the houses during Christmas vacation and reading it in one sitting when I should have been working on a term paper. That made me a Jane Austen fan for life!

May 1958—Bill accepted the job as manager of Person Farms poultry processing plant in Roxboro. The family moved when they found a house. (This was in the 1958 Christmas Letter.)

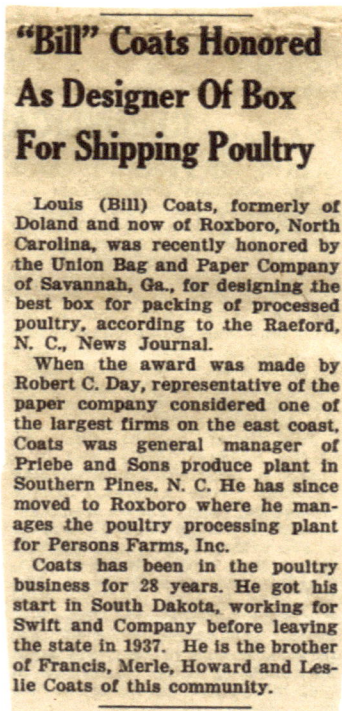

ROXBORO, NORTH CAROLINA
JULY 1958–SPRING 1961

Doug graduated from high school here.

31 July 1958: "Bill Coats Honored As Designer of Box For Shipping Poultry," appeared on page one of the *Doland* (S.D.) *Times-Record*. Also, a photo of Bill receiving the award was in the *News Journal* (Raeford, NC) on 3 April 1958.

In October 1958, Bill spent two weeks in the local hospital being treated for a duodenal ulcer (per the 1958 Christmas Letter).

—**1212 Oxford Road.** According to Donna, "We lived a few miles out of town in a small, one-story house. I took the bus to school every day. I think that house had only three bedrooms

---

"Bill" Coats Honored As Designer Of Box For Shipping Poultry

Louis (Bill) Coats, formerly of Doland and now of Roxboro, North Carolina, was recently honored by the Union Bag and Paper Company of Savannah, Ga., for designing the best box for packing of processed poultry, according to the Raeford, N. C., News Journal.

When the award was made by Robert C. Day, representative of the paper company considered one of the largest firms on the east coast, Coats was general manager of Priebe and Sons produce plant in Southern Pines, N. C. He has since moved to Roxboro where he manages the poultry processing plant for Persons Farms, Inc.

Coats has been in the poultry business for 28 years. He got his start in South Dakota, working for Swift and Company before leaving the state in 1937. He is the brother of Francis, Merle, Howard and Leslie Coats of this community.

The Times-Record, Doland, S.D., 31 Julyl 1958, page 1.

and you and I shared, as well as Doug and Dave shared. Of course, that wasn't really an issue since we weren't home together much. We first met Alan in Roxboro. I remember playing bridge in the living room of that house with you and Alan. I used to get up early in the morning and play casino with Dad. He probably was in a gambling phase at that time. When we left Roxboro in the spring, I remember feeling like we were slinking out of town. They owed money to everyone. I saw a list Mother had typed up of all the people to whom they owed money, including my music teacher."

David recalled that he just "visited a couple of times while in college and the service. Ugh." I do have one good story about Doug from there though. David said he "worked there one summer and also met the brother of Hall of Famer Enos 'Country' Slaughter." *David—please tell us the Doug story!*

Donna also remembered Roxboro was the place where "the dawning of my awareness of Mother and Dad's problems occurred. It seems to me that Mother had a very depressed period here. I really cannot think of anything good from that era."

Deane: I remember that Ouida had several falls, which may have contributed to the depressed period Donna remembers. Ouida fell on the brick stoop at the house and was laid up a good while. Then she also had a fall at someone else's house that laid her up again. She thought she was opening the bathroom door but opened the basement door instead while she was talking to someone behind her, and down the stairs she went. Once while I was there an insurance man came to settle the claim for one of the accidents. I remember it because she did not ask for much and he was offering her more, perhaps to make sure she didn't come back for more later! And there were plenty of other problems to depress Ouida. Bill was gambling again and had to borrow money to pay off his losses. Then, when he took the next job, he didn't even tell her. He told me and relied on me to tell her. I did not want to do his dirty work but felt that my mother needed to know as soon as possible so I told her.

Ouida herself, in the 1960 Christmas letter, wrote: "1960 was not her year! Two falls have, during the year, kept her sitting with one or the other leg propped on a pillow." The letter did not mention any other problems.

Deane: I also remember the bridge games there. It seems that that was the last time everyone was home at the same time, and we all made it several times. We had a rotating bridge game, so that when one got up another one sat down and started playing. Memories of those visits are for the most part pleasant. Donna had a taffy pull for a birthday party here. I was home and helped with it—it went well, but everywhere was sticky when it was over.

In the 1961 Christmas letter, Ouida wrote, "In February 1961, Bill took a new job, manager of the FCX Poultry Processing Plant in Hiddenite, N.C. The town was named after a man named Hidden who discovered a gemstone found only in this area."

TAYLORSVILLE, NORTH CAROLINA
MAY–JULY 1961.

Taylorsville was about six miles from the plant.

They were there very briefly. Donna said, "They yanked me out of school in Roxboro just before the end of the year and made me start 6th grade in Taylorsville. We lived in that house out in the country in Taylorsville for a few months, and then all of a sudden we were in Hiddenite." Before they moved into the Taylorsville house, they "stayed one weekend in the 'minus 5-star' Taylorsville Hotel. Eichmann was on trial, and I recall watching it on the TV in that rickety old hotel. Our house of a few months was about a mile outside town and was two stories."

HIDDENITE, NORTH CAROLINA
JULY 1961–SUMMER 1966

Unless otherwise noted all the Hiddenite notes come from Donna.

October 1961—"Bill started another plant, this one in Lexington, N.C., to freeze and pack poultry. Between Hiddenite and Lexington, he finds that he stays very busy!" (1961 Christmas letter.)

January 1962—"Chicken Dinners for Western Europe" was the title of an article in *Carolina Co-operator*, p. 9, published by FCX. It mentioned two projects under Bill's direct supervision. This article describes what the two plants were doing cooperatively.

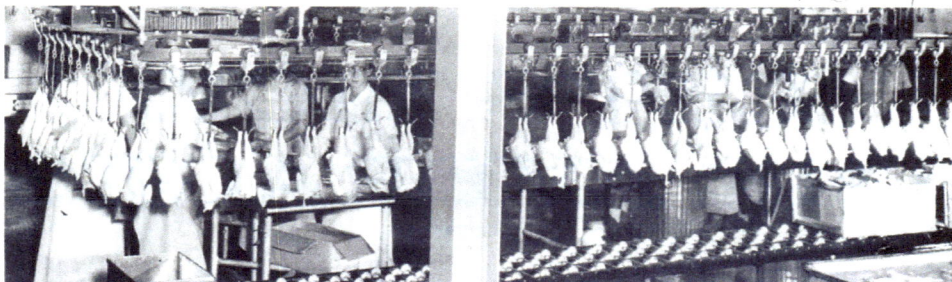

Assembly-line techniques allow a relatively few workers to prepare for shipment overseas as much as 30,000 pounds of poultry every day. The birds move quickly through the FCX plant at Lexington, on their way to the export market.

CHICKEN DINNERS for WESTERN EUROPE

Through a far-reaching cooperative undertaking, poultry is now moving from Carolina farms to dinner tables in western Europe as well as to school lunch programs and other markets that are closer to home.

CAROLINA broilers are showing up on dinner tables in western Europe these days thanks largely to what almost amounts to an all-co-op operation.

In a Lexington, N. C., plant leased last October, FCX is now processing and freezing poultry for shipment to West Germany and other European countries. In the Lexington operation, FCX is able to carry its poultry processing one step closer to the actual consumer of food grown here in the Carolinas. At the cooperative's plant in Hiddenite, birds are dressed and then shipped to Lexington where they are prepared for export.

Both operations are under the direct supervision of L. D. Coats, manager of the Hiddenite plant since February, 1960. He has had 23 years of experience in poultry processing work.

FCX acquired the Hiddenite plant in January of 1960, thus achieving a fully integrated broiler operation for Carolina farmers. With their own processing plant, farmers could provide their own services from the time chicks were put in until they arrived at the market, ready for the consumer's table. The plant processes about 40,000 birds a day.

Part of the dressed birds are iced down and shipped in wire baskets from Hiddenite to the Lexington plant, where they are placed in polyethylene bags—which mold themselves to the birds and cling tightly when air is removed through a vacuum process.

After being placed in the plastic bags, the birds are packed in boxes of 12, quick frozen, and then held in storage until shipped. Most of the birds are being shipped overseas through Charleston, S. C.

At both Hiddenite and Lexington, federal inspectors are present in the plants at all times during working hours. Every bird leaving the plants is inspected for wholesomeness.

Under government contract, the Lexington plant also supplies cut-up birds for the federal school lunch program. Most of these are for use in North Carolina schools.

The 25 workers in Lexington are processing and freezing between 25,000 and 30,000 pounds per day. James W. Mastin, who joined FCX in August of last year, is plant manager. He has 12 years of poultry operations experience.

The North American Poultry Cooperative Association acts as selling agent for this project. The organization serves a number of cooperatives from Maine to Mississippi. The regional office which works with FCX is located in Charlotte.

The polyethylene bags in which the birds are packed adhere closely to the birds, forming a kind of protective "second skin" during the final processing and freezing before shipment from the cooperative's plant to various parts of Europe.

(published by FCX)

—House across from the gym, one year.

—House near B. M. Miller's store, four years.

Donna: "We lived in Hiddenite from the time I entered the 7th grade through the 11th grade (1961-1966), five long years. Doug had gone off to college, so I was the only child left at home with Mother and Dad. It seemed to me, and I certainly believed, that Mother thought that Hiddenite was the most backward of towns in which we had lived."

"We lived one year in the house across from the school gymnasium, and then we moved up to the house a couple of doors from BM Miller's store where we lived until the summer of 1966. I went to Salem College for Governor's School that summer with no idea that I wouldn't be returning to Hiddenite."

Both houses "were one-story brick houses. Each was three-bedrooms and had one bath. I liked the second house. I spent most of my time in what we called the music room. It had a wonderful blue velvet sofa with high arms and a high back that had been left in the house by previous tenants or the owner. It was very comfortable to drape oneself all over the sofa and read. Miss Otie lived next door on one side, and the other house had outdoor plumbing. I still remember Dad cutting the hedge in the back (now that's a shocker—he actually did some yard work) and stopping when he realized it would expose the outdoor john. There was a garage that had a small apartment up above it, but I don't think we ever used the apartment for anything. Dad always came home and sat in the backroom where the TV was and fell asleep. Mother spent all her time in the living room, reading in her rocking chair until late in the evening when she moved to the back room and watched Johnny Carson (or was it Jack Paar at that time?)."

"One early recollection is being disappointed to discover that there was no public library in Alexander County. We found the public library in Statesville and made a stop at the library a part of our weekly visits to Statesville to buy groceries. Those Saturday trips with Mother to Statesville or Hickory to buy groceries and visit the library were weekly highlights. We often stopped to have lunch at Little Pig after shopping at the A&P Grocery Store.

"As I recall, when we first lived in Hiddenite, Mother did not have a car of her own. It is hard to remember whether she took Dad to work and had the use of the car during the day or whether she was stranded. She did get her first car in Hiddenite. I cannot remember what that first car was; was it a Chevy II?" Doug remembers that the folks first got a second car in Roxboro—1958-59. "It was a black '55 Dodge, followed by a '61 Dodge Lancer which was passed on to me my senior year in college"

Christmas 1962. The Coats family and Deane's husband,
Alan Dierksen, on the far right in back row.

OUIDA GOES BACK TO SCHOOL.

Deane: Ouida attended Huron College for three years, dropping out when she and Bill were married in 1933. Her parents had been educators and badly wanted their children to finish college. Bess Moulton once commented to me that Ouida's father had cried when she quit college to get married. Fast-forward to the 1960s—Ouida now wanted to get her degree. With a loan from her mother, she enrolled at Lenoir Rhyne College in Hickory, North Carolina. She had lots of eight o'clock classes and was a little nervous about being a student after so many years. But everything went well, and she graduated in August 1963. I

Ouida Coats at graduation from Lenoir Rhyne College, Hiclory, N.C., August 1963.

rather enjoyed the fact of her eight o'clock classes because she'd had no sympathy for me the semester that I had six eight o'clock classes.

In a letter to her mother on 1 May 1964, Ouida said: "I guess if I had not moved to Hiddenite and been bored stiff, I probably would not have had the nerve to go on and finish college so I could get some kind of work that would interest me. You know that I inquired twice before at various colleges but chickened out before I did anything about it." [Original in Deane's files.]

Donna: "It was a great boon when Mother decided to return to school and get her college degree at Lenoir Rhyne College in Hickory. She was more animated and involved than she had been in some time. I remember spending one summer in Boone, N.C., while Mother took classes at Appalachian State College. Mother was determined that I take tennis lessons because I think she wanted me to have a few opportunities that were not readily available in Alexander County. That summer must have been when I was 15, because I recall Dad visiting one weekend and taking me out for a drive with my learners permit. Mother's car was manual shift and there were lots of hills. We had a VERY rough ride, and I think Dad was mortified. When we got home at the end of the summer, he bought a Chevy Malibu with automatic shift. That was the first car that I really got to drive.

"Mother became the school librarian at Hiddenite School. I felt strange at first having her at the school, but it became OK. It was definitely a big boon for her to have a job and some money of her own. I remember her making plans to take one of her first foreign trips during summer vacation and then having to cancel it because she had lung surgery. It makes me sad to think of that time because it seemed like several steps forward for her (graduating, getting a job, making plans to travel), and then getting batted down by health problems."

In the fall of 1965, Ouida's mother said Ouida "enrolled in an Extension course by [television] from the university. It's after school three nights a week until Dec. 17. It gives her the needed hours to be certified in Library Science & get the A certificate. It gives her

$70 more per month pay, as she gets $50 less because of B certificate and $20 is taken off because she's not teaching in her certified field of English & History." (Excerpt from a letter from Bess Moulton to Irene Adermann, 21 September 1965. Original in Deane's files.)

Deane's memory: In early 1966, Ouida had lung surgery because of something suspicious on an x-ray. It turned out to be a calcified tuberculosis lesion (or something like that), not cancer. After a period of recuperation, she went back to work. Because she still was not up to par, she was not able to come when my daughter Marianne was born 19 April 1966. At some earlier time, Ouida had said that when she was young, maybe high school, and very thin, her parents worried that she had tuberculosis. It took Ouida some time to recover completely from this surgery. In a letter 16 May 1966 to her brother Jasper and his wife, she said, "My recovery comes slowly but surely—so slow it irks me, but that I can't help." She went on to say, "I may still go to Europe—but it will be after July 20th & a short trip. I still tire so easily—want to wait & see about how I feel. I'd hate to spend my dough and be too tired all the time to see anything." (Copy of letter in Deane's files.)

Ouida in her job at the Hiddenite school library, October 1964.

Donna: "At some point in writing about Hiddenite, I need to write about music—about Floyd Cramer, Kay Starr, West Side Story, Sound of Music, and a lot of the records we listened to. I do have vivid memories of playing all those records and hearing them over and over again. The other night I caught a few minutes of the country music awards show [1998]. In it they did a segment of country music greats who died during the past year. Floyd Cramer was one of those (d. Dec. 1997], and they played some of his best known songs which were VERY familiar to me."

David's notes on Hiddenite: "Clearer memories here. I only visited them in Taylorsville once. Visited many times here, and they were here when I got out of the service. Remember in Roxboro you [Deane] and a boyfriend (think the same one in NY) coming to pick me

up and having car trouble. He was perplexed and embarrassed but had just flooded it. Remember Alan in Hiddenite and his pictures and getting the family drunk with his Scarlett O'Hara drinks. Especially Doug and Dad. Terrible mixture—I went with him to buy the rotgut he used. Got out of the service while they lived here and worked for a few months in Statesville before moving to Kentucky."

STATESVILLE, NORTH CAROLINA
25 JULY 1966-JUNE 1967

Donna graduated from high school here.

On 22 July 1966, Ouida sent a postcard Jasper Moulton and family: "Just a note to let you know we are moving to Statesville N.C. (124 Bost St.) this coming Monday. It is a town 15 miles from here of 16,000. We will be nearer shopping, doctors and hospitals, golf courses, etc., etc. Our new phone no. is 873-8792. We commute to jobs." This was just a few weeks after Ouida had moved her mother from Buffalo, Minnesota, to live with her in Hiddenite.

Ouida in school library, January 1967.

—124 **Bost Street**. Deane: This was another big house—I recall an upstairs hallway that was almost large enough to be a sitting room. Alan and I and the children spent Thanksgiving 1966 there. I have photos of us with our grandmother Bess Moulton in the living room there. One background feature is the white fiberglass draperies with tree branches on them—they were present in Coats family homes for many years. Also visible is that sectional sofa that was always moving apart, never very satisfactory but they had it for years. My children (then ages one and three) and I went down to stay with Donna and Bess in March 1967 when Ouida went to California for Doug and Helen's wedding. Bess asked me whether I had the baby trained yet—this stuck in my mind because I didn't have the first baby trained yet (though he trained himself very shortly thereafter!).

Donna relates: "All of a sudden they had moved to Statesville, and Dad no longer worked for Holly Farms. I never have known what happened with that. Grandma came to live with us, and I did my senior year at Statesville High School. Dad was gone most of the year working in Lumberton and possibly one or two other places. It was a pretty miserable year. Dad was home only on weekends and he sniped at Grandma all the time."

"We had a two-story house with two bedrooms downstairs. One was for Mother and the other was for Grandma. Upstairs there was a large hallway that could have served as a den. There were two bedrooms—one was mine and the other was Dad's on the weekends. My room had a little second room. This house was in Statesville—not out in the country. It wasn't that far from the A&P and Little Pig BBQ that we had visited for years on Saturdays when mother drove to Statesville from Hiddenite to buy groceries and we always ate lunch at Little Pig. I certainly remember the movie theater in Statesville. That is where we went to the movies from Hiddenite. It had an entrance in the front for whites and an entrance in the back for blacks who sat up in the balcony."

In May 1967, Bill's oldest brother, Leslie Coats, and Leslie's wife, Roslea, who still lived in South Dakota, visited, perhaps on their way to Florida. We never saw Bill's family very much once we left South Dakota, and especially after we moved to North Carolina.

Four generations, including Ouida, her mother Bess Moulton, my two children, and me, Thanksgiving 1966.

The May 1967 visit of Les & Roslea, at left, with Ouida and Bill.

ROSE HILL, NORTH CAROLINA
BEGINNING JUNE 1967 FOR ONLY A FEW MONTHS.

In a letter to Irene and Jasper, dated 9 May [1967], Ouida said, "Bill has rented us a house in Rose Hill, and we will be moving sometime between the 10th and the 15th of June. We got a three-bedroom house with 1½ baths so there will be room for Mother if she decides to come back." She commented that the house was on one floor with electric heat and that it "sounds nice from what Bill tells us about it, and Donna and I are going to Rose Hill this coming Saturday to see. We want to be able to know where our furniture will fit in and how much of it we will have to sell, give, or throw away. We have had 8 and 9 room houses for the past 5 years so I imagine we will have to get rid of some stuff."

Donna's recalled: "We moved to Rose Hill a few days after I graduated. I only spent a few days to a week there. I cannot recall exactly what I did that summer, but I wonder if I spent it with Deane and Alan. Is that the summer that I worked as a cashier at a cafeteria in Washington? I don't really remember but I know I only spent a few days in Rose Hill, but Mother and Dad were there for the summer." *[I think 1967 must be the summer Donna stayed with us and worked at a government cafeteria somewhere in Arlington or DC. I don't remember how she got to work from our house. DD]*

RAMSEUR, NORTH CAROLINA
SEPTEMBER–DECEMBER 1967

Donna has "just the vaguest of memories of Ramseur. I don't think I was in Ramseur but twice (possibly only once), and I don't think I was there at the same time as your family. It was a little one-story house in a neighborhood with paved streets, but not the smooth city streets—more that pebbly asphalt type paving that is in the outskirts. It was brick. I think I was only there once, and they probably weren't there more than a period of months. I have a mental picture of the house, but I'm finding it hard to write a decent description." On another occasion Donna said: "I think I went to Ramseur for Thanksgiving, but by Christmas, I think they were in Salisbury."

Deane: This sounds like the house that I remember visiting probably only once. I only remember it at all because of an incident involving my children and a locked door. The house was small, only one story, and situated on ground that sloped down in the back. The children were quite young—Elliott was three and one-half and Marianne was one and one-half. They were to sleep in a back corner bedroom that was way higher than ground level. After dark, when Marianne was asleep, Elliot came out of the room and somehow locked the door on his way out. The folks hadn't been there long, had no key to the room, and we couldn't get it open. If they had a ladder it wasn't long enough to reach the window, but probably they didn't have one. At any event, we had to call the landlord for help. Alan remembers that the landlord had some kind of key that went into the center of the doorknob and would unlock that kind of (unkeyed) lock. Since our house in Fairlington had the same kind of locks, Alan got a key like that as soon as we got home.

Bill & Ouida, Christmas 1967.

Based on Donna's comment above, Bill and Ouida probably celebrated Christmas in Salisbury, not Ramseur, in December 1967. Their photo shows them holding photos of presents from Doug and me: on the right—Doug and Helen's wedding photo; on the left two photos of my family and me; and on the wall on the right a nut wreath that I made.

SALISBURY, MARYLAND
DECEMBER 1967-JUNE 1968

—**211 Walston Avenue**. Deane: They were there less than a year. Ouida left her teaching job in N.C. and took a teaching job in Salisbury midyear. They had a very small house there, with no bedroom for Donna. Ouida was very unhappy about that. Bess was with them at this point. I remember driving their car over to Salisbury when we still lived on South Buchanan Street in Arlington. Why I had it I am not sure, but I definitely remember driving it over the Chesapeake Bay Bridge.

Information about Bill's job and the company he worked for in Siler City as it appeared in the book *Chatham County 1771-1971*:

> In 1969, the value of poultry and eggs produced in Chatham County ($26,145,400) was more than the value of poultry and eggs produced in the entire state in 1910, 1920 and 1925.[15]

In the section on Mid-State Farms:

> In 1956 Mr. and Mrs. E. T. Watson of Raleigh purchased the processing plant of Siler City Poultry Exchange and operated it as Watson's Poultry Company until June, 1965. At that time, Watson Poultry Company merged with Holt Milling Company and Alamance Broiler Service forming Mid-State Farms Cooperative Company. Of the total 230 employees, 185 are employed in the processing division in Siler City. L. D. Coats is manager of this division.[16]

In 1969, Bill was diagnosed with diverticulitis. His progress is noted in family letters (the originals are in Deane's files):

- **April 21:** Bess Moulton to Jasper Moulton: Had letters from Irene and Ouida last week. Bill has been quite sick but is able to play golf already, and didn't have to have an operation.

- **April 27:** Ouida to Jasper: Bill is much better and will probably not have to have an operation but is on a strict diet and has lost too much weight too fast and is tired all the time. One knows he doesn't feel too hot as he doesn't play golf only once in a while and then doesn't play as long as usual.

- **May 27:** Ouida to her mother, Bess: Bill has had a setback and is in the hospital again. The Drs. think his intestine has opened again but are hopeful that he can

---

15 Wade Hampton Hadley, Doris Goerch Horton, and Nell Craig Strowd, *Chatham County 1771-1971,* Chatham County Historical Assn. (Charlotte, N.C.: Delmar Printing Co., 1976), 380.

16 Hadley, et al., *Chatham County 1771-1971,* 387.

come thru without an operation. They do feel that he will eventually have to have the operation, but if they can stop the infection first it will be much less serious.

Deane, Alan, Donna, and Bill. Christmas 1969.

- **June 10:** Ouida to Jasper, Marilyn, and all: Bill has spent another week in the hospital but is out now, trying to get up strength and keep from having another attack before July when he will have the injured intestinal piece removed by surgery. This is so much better than having to have a series of three operations, which they first projected. I'm leaving day after tomorrow (by car) for Buffalo [Minnesota] for a 10-day stay. Both Bill and his Drs. said it was okay for me to leave now—better than after his surgery. He goes to the office several hours per day now—plays a little golf by riding carts—just has to rest lots and keep on his diet.

- **September 14:** Ouida to Bess: Bill gets better & feels stronger every day. He's thinking of going back to work the latter part of next week—at least for half days. I'll bet he'll be back playing golf in another month.

He looked well in a Christmas photo in December 1969.

- **30 August 1970:** Bill had a mild heart attack. On 2 October, Ouida wrote to Jasper and Marilyn Moulton:

  . . . He spent two weeks in the hospital—and is on his third week home—resting and recovering. The Dr. wants him to spend this week and next still doing nothing much—and then will let him go back to work part-time for one more month before he can work full time. Tells him he will be as good as new then and will probably live longer than if he'd not had this warning to slow down. We're very pleased with his progress, and he is feeling so good that it is hard for him to not do things. (Original letter in Deane's files.)

—510 West Cardinal Street, 1968–1970. Deane: This was a centrally located, large, older brick house near downtown, next door to Selma and Francis Grimes. The folks rented it, and by 28 February 1970 the owners had evidently decided to sell it. Ouida's letter to her mother of that date noted: "They have not had a single person want to buy the house yet so we may not have to move till later. Can stay till June anyway."

One afternoon during a visit there, my daughter Marianne went missing—she was probably two or three. We searched everywhere in the house—under the beds, in the closets, every place we could think of, then started searching the neighborhood. Panic set in after a while because there was small pond or wading pool in the park near the house. But she wasn't there—and we were on the point of calling the police when we decided to search the house again. This time we found her, asleep under her bed but right up against the wall, crosswise under the head of the bed. That's why we missed her the first time. Of course, there was great relief and rejoicing all around. This generated so much attention that Elliot tried the same thing a day or two later. What a surprise he got when everyone got angry with him for doing the same thing!

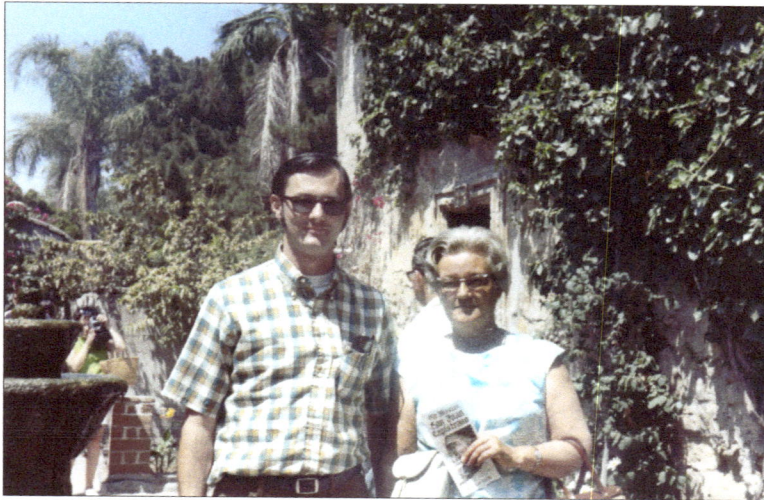

Doug and Ouida Coats, July 1970, San Juan Capistrano.

—North Garden Avenue, 1970–1971. Deane: I am not sure of the house number as it is not given in the deed. On the plat map, it is on the southwest corner of Driftwood and North Garden; the next corner going away from U.S. 64 is Cliftwood. The house number must have been in the 800 or 900 block. The folks bought it in June 1970; it was a brick, ranch-style, one-story house with three bedrooms, two baths.[17]

David remembers it as "a nice little house with a carport." The folks used a post office box, PO Box 244, beginning by 3 August 1970, the date on one of Ouida's letters; they probably got it when they moved to this house. David and Kathy bought this house from them when they moved to Siler City in late August or early September 1971; the deed is dated March 1972. Neighbors David remembers

17 Chatham County, North Carolina, Chatham County Deed Records, Book 353:84, L. D. and Ouida Coats, purchase Garden Avenue property, 19 June 1970; Chatham County Court House, Pittsboro, North Carolina.

are the Hughes family who lived behind this house and John Etchison, a local bank president, who lived next door. David and Kathy didn't live here long, later moving to another house in Siler City before going on to Florida.

Ouida got to take at least one trip in 1970, to California, when Doug took her to San Juan Capistrano.

In March 1971, Ouida's mother, Bessie (Sturges) Moulton died in Buffalo, Minnesota. Ouida and her siblings, (Royal) Jasper "Jay" Moulton and Irene Adermann, were there for the funeral, and they took care of as many details of the house and estate as they had time for. Bess's younger sister, Myra (Sturges) Little, who lived in Buffalo, probably took care of a number of the details. Myra had been a tremendous help to Bess many times during her last years.

—Pine Forest Drive, Lot 53, Pine Forest II, 1971–1978/79. Deane: By 7 September 1971, the folks had moved into the house they built that backed up to the golf course. In a letter Ouida wrote to Irene and Jasper on that date she said, "My luck held and we did have to move into the new house on the day the teachers started to school [probably late August]. The yard, driveway etc. had had nothing done to them, but the inside of the house is done and we are living in it." Why they built this house so soon after buying the Garden Avenue house is not known, but a guess would be that the money Ouida inherited from her mother, who died in March 1971, was a factor (the part Bill didn't lose by investing unsuccessfully in scotch whiskey!).[18]

Ouida, Jasper, and Irene. March 1971.

Leslie, Bill (Louis), Shorty (Ron), Francis, Howard Coats - 1972.

18 Bessie S. Moulton Probate file, Wright County file #10790, Wright County Courthouse, Buffalo, Minnesota, Buffalo, Minnesota, 1971–1972. Ouida's one-third share was $14,852.14 less tax of $177.04 and $1,000 borrowed 4 January 1963 netted $13,675.10. Not sure whether that included the two houses Bessie owned.

In 1972, Bill got together with four of his six brothers, probably in South Dakota. The two missing brothers are Maurice "Sid" and Merle. They had one sister, Norma (Coats) Thomas.

In the 1972 Christmas letter, Ouida noted she "got pushed into being a remedial reading teacher this year besides coordinating the library. A most rewarding job but the library is still her first love." In the 1973 Christmas letter, Ouida said she "finally realized her dream and went to Europe this past summer. A 'Grand' or 'see as much as you can in the time-allotted' type tour."

1974 Christmas letter:

- June—Ouida took a trip to Hawaii, "toured four islands and had a ball." While on the beach, Ouida ran into a woman she had met and become friends with in Europe in 1973.

- May—Bill "hit the high of his golfing career. Won a Scratch Golf Tournament in the N.C. Mountains—placed 1st out of 128 entries. The large Trophy was presented by Miss America (Rebecca Jean King). Missed the Hawaiian trip in order to direct a crash program for the Company to fight recession. It was hectic but very profitable."

- August—Ouida took a reading workshop at Appalachian S. U. She noted later that her work was made easier with the help of a full-time aide and the reading course.

1975 Christmas letter:
- Ouida made a "three-week tour of Norway, Sweden, Finland, Russia, and Denmark which she enjoyed in spite of bursitis in her right heel."

1976 Christmas letter:
- Ouida traveled to the Bahamas and Britain.

1977 Christmas letter:
- Ouida noted trips to Egypt (seven days), an Aegean cruise with a stop in Istanbul. "Super tour except for a few days of the "Pharaoh's Curse. . . History really comes alive when seeing all those antiquities."

- Another comment was that "Bill has four difficult months ahead before complete retirement. This will make 48 years of active work in the Poultry Industry—plus 2 part-time years in high school with Glen 'Cy' Lovelace grading eggs, etc."

In 1978, they purchased 1005 North Garden, near 10th and Homewood Acres. They may have planned to rent it out.[19]

—502 Greenhill Drive, about 1979-1982. This was their home at the time of Ouida's death. It was a smaller house than the one they built on the golf course. They probably moved there after one or both retired. Ouida retired in 1978; her principal enforced mandatory retirement at age 65. Ouida wanted to teach one more year because it would improve her pension and was unhappy that he wouldn't agree to it. My guess is that he didn't have the authority to do it, even if he wanted to. Bill retired about the same year.

Both parents smoked and continued smoking throughout most of my childhood. At some point, probably around the time she retired, Ouida stopped smoking through hypnotism. Unfortunately, she stopped too late to prevent lung cancer. I am not aware that she had ever previously tried to stop. Bill smoked, too, although he stopped several times for several years each time—not sure whether he was smoking toward the end of his life.

From a short 1980 Christmas note:

- Ouida took a 23-day tour of the Orient in May.

- This summer Ouida decided to take up lap swimming and when September came, she and a buddie [sic] joined the YMCA in a small city near here where [they] swim at least three times a week. It is such good exercise for her arthritic legs and feet. [I remember her saying their goal was to swim 100 miles.]

- Bill has also been on several golf weekends—one in February at Myrtle Beach, S.C., and in July at Southern Pines where he shot a record! He shot his age (70) one day and two under the next day.

---

19 Chatham County, North Carolina, Chatham County Deed Records, Book 418:774, L. D. & Ouida Coats purchased Lot 1005, North Garden Avenue, 11 December 1978; Chatham County Court House, Pittsboro, N.C.

Early in 1981, Ouida's doctor wanted her to have tests to determine the cause of pain in her leg or hip. She decided to defer this until after her planned trip by car to California. She had some pain pills with her but they were not sufficient. Donna remembers "going to Tijuana with Mother, Doug, and Helen (and I thought Dad) to a jai alai game. After the game, we had to walk to the car and mother was in intense pain. Those moments of trying to get her back to the car and back home are seared in my mind." Fortunately, Helen, who must have realized what a serious situation this was, somehow got a prescription from her family doctor for more pills for Ouida. Doug remembers that the medication was Vicodin.

June 1981 reunion at Donna's in California. Standing, left to right: David and Doug; seated, left to right: Donna and Deane.

The trip back to North Carolina was extremely difficult because of Ouida's pain. I thought Bill had to fly out to drive her home, but Donna recalls that he was already with her. Soon after she got home, she was diagnosed with bone cancer that had metastasized from a lung cancer; she was treated at North Carolina Memorial Hospital in Chapel Hill.

Bill wrote a letter to the "Coats Klan" on 15 April 1981: Ouida was to go to North Carolina Memorial Hospital in Chapel Hill that day. He described the treatment she was getting and promised that he would keep "all our family. . . equally informed." I think he followed through on that after an initial period of being too upset to make much sense. He sent a second letter on 18 October 1961 that mentioned the family reunion over Labor Day and the T-shirts that Donna brought. He summarized Ouida's treatment and said she was stable at the time. Both these letters were among those that Betty Brown sent me.

All in all, Bill took excellent care of Ouida during her final year. And she noticed. During the September 1981 family reunion, she commented to me to that she never thought her marriage could improve like it had. All four children plus two spouses were there, and everyone was on their best behavior. Ouida had divided all the family photos into four packets, one for each of us. Donna brought reunion T-shirts for everybody. Doug brought the wine he had set aside for Ouida and Bill's 50th anniversary— Ouida commented that was because he knew they wouldn't make to their fiftieth. At that point they had been married forty-eight years.

The whole Coats group at September 1981 reunion: back row, Deane, David, and Doug; middle row, Donna, Kathy, and Helen; seated, Ouida and Bill.

Coats women, standing, left to right, Donna, Helen, and Kathy; seated, left to right, Ouida and Deane. September 1981 reunion.

Ouida did get to see her siblings before she died. Her sister Irene had come from Minnesota for about a month in the spring. In October, Ouida and Bill drove to Florida to visit David and his family in Kissimmee. David has photos from that visit. While there, they visited Ouida's brother, Jasper Moulton, in Indialantic. On the way back to David's, a deer ran into them and their car was totaled. They were uninjured, and Ouida commented that she didn't survive everything that had happened up to that point to get killed by a deer! She had quit smoking several years earlier, but as David noted, "When she knew she was on a short leash, she started smoking again."

Jasper and Ouida, October 1981.

Ouida's obit, from unknown newspaper (perhaps the Siler City newspaper?).

At Christmas, Ouida and Bill flew to California to spend the holiday with Doug and Helen and Donna and Chuck. Doug remembers that Bill bought Ouida a white blouse for Christmas. On New Year's Day in San Diego, she had a brain hemorrhage as the result of the blood thinner she had been taking. She was admitted to Mercy Hospital in San Diego, where it was soon discovered that her lung tumor had recurred. She spent almost a month in the hospital before going back to Donna's home where she died on 9 February 1982. She was cremated and her ashes scattered at sea off the coast of San Diego. She had always said she wished to be cremated because she thought funerals, especially with open caskets, were barbaric. On the Friday after her death, we all gathered at an overlook at the Pacific Ocean. As we watched, a ship left with the week's ashes, scattering flowers on the water on its way out to sea where the ashes were scattered.

After Ouida's funeral, the immediate family went to Donna's house and is shown here in Donna's backyard.

On the day Ouida died, Bill wrote Myra Little, her favorite aunt, with the news. He said he had planned to call, but when he learned that she was in the hospital, he decided it was best to write.[20]

---

20 Ray Little papers, viewed August 1999.

GENERAL COMMENTS ON THE PARENTS.

OUIDA WAS THE MORE RESPONSIBLE PARENT, although one could describe her as hypercritical, not warm and fuzzy. But she provided a stable and organized home life with regular meals on a regular schedule, clean clothes, etc., and *she was there*.

In many ways she was "hands off"—I often wished for more guidance and support. There were times, though, when she went to bat for one of us. For me, it was her battle to get me into the proper grade after Perry wouldn't let me enter first grade. Mostly, if I complained about a sibling or anyone else, her response was, "What did you do to provoke him/her/them?" That may have been a phrase used by many parents during that era, but I didn't know that then. I do know that from childhood on I never wanted to share my feelings with her.

We also know that Bill worked very hard at his job, had an excellent work reputation, and always seemed able to find another comparable or better job. He started out at the bottom, so to speak, of the poultry business and steadily moved to more responsible positions, ending up as manager of several good-sized poultry plants. In response to my question about whether he had done any public or community service, David commented in an email on 31 December 2003: "He was on the Siler City hospital board. Also on board at country club. I think he was one time president of national poultry possessors [processors] assn. (hazy about that but [he] did have some high position)." Doug guessed (via telecon 3 January 2004) that it was at Hiddenite and that he was not president, but held some other office of whatever the group was. Doris didn't know about it but checked with a close friend of Bill's who thought it probably was true. I was unable to confirm this because I don't know the name of the organization. And I don't recall ever being told about Bill's accomplishments—and now I wonder why.

It was typical then for family life to revolve around the father/breadwinner and his habits. That was certainly the case here—our family life revolved around Bill, his work, and his athletic activities (mostly golf). He controlled the TV and the car when there was only one of each. After we left Perry, he changed jobs and moved the family fairly often, apparently without any consideration of the impact on family members. It seemed to me that Ouida's reaction to the moves was that it was our job to adjust. If it was hard for us, then we were at fault. How much of that was typical of the times? Probably some of it was. But it was hard on me and probably on all of us. The three older children and perhaps Donna as well all felt like we never fit in.

One thing that was, one hopes, not so typical, was how Bill handled money in his and the family's personal life. As far as I could tell, he never planned anything, especially where money was involved; that included savings, vacations, college. At times he gambled and had to deal with debts to the detriment of family expenses. On his general attitude on money, Ouida often said he had the farmer mentality—a farmer worked all year on borrowed money and paid it back when the crops came in. She never mentioned in my hearing anything about gambling debts. In general, she defended him to the children or didn't say anything. One other thing I remember about money is that when we moved to North Carolina, Bill did not pay the state income tax for some years. Somehow he must have thought he wouldn't be caught. But eventually he was caught, perhaps before we left Concord. I do not have any more details on this.

Bill played favorites. David was always first on his list. That did not do David any favor, but it took me till middle age to realize that. Donna was second, then first, when the rest of us were gone and she was like an only child. I was third on the list and Doug was last. He took a lot of guff from Bill over the years.

Both Bill and Ouida drank, sometimes to excess. I wasn't aware of any problems with Bill's drinking until Concord. There, when he had had too much to drink, he was sometimes sloppy sentimental. Ugh! Donna could probably comment more on Ouida's drinking as it was mostly after I was grown. On visits I did notice that when she had had a good bit of beer, her drink of choice, she made pronouncements punctuated by a sound with her lower lip.

Donna's comments on the parents (email to DD, 11/26/2020): "I think each of our experiences was different and mine, in particular, because I was the only one at home for years. Neither of them came to plays or athletic events in which I was involved. When I see the involvement of friends of ours in their children and grandchildren's lives, it seems very different from our experience. I don't think they set a good example for us of marriage as a partnership between two loving adults. I never saw much affection between them. I remember wondering why mother stayed married to him though now I intellectually understand the social and economic strictures [that] bound her. Dad did stick by her and care for her through her final illness."

In the end, whatever they did or didn't do, all four of us managed somehow to grow up and become self-supporting and reasonably productive citizens. As we have gotten older, we have had a number of sibling reunions. Here are photos from most of them. We did have a reunion in 2019 in Savannah, but I don't have any photos from that one.

Coats gang rides into Tahoe, November 1985. Back row, left to right: Donna, David, Deane; seated: Doug.

2 November 1986 at Doug's wedding. Left to right: Deane, Doug, Donna, and David.

1996 reunion, in Virginia, at Deane's.
Pictured left to right, Donna, Doug, David, and Deane.

October 1999 reunion, in Florida, at David's, celebrating two
birthdays: Donna, age 50, and David, age 60.

We included more people at this reunion: our two half-brothers,
Dennis on the left and Rodney on the right.

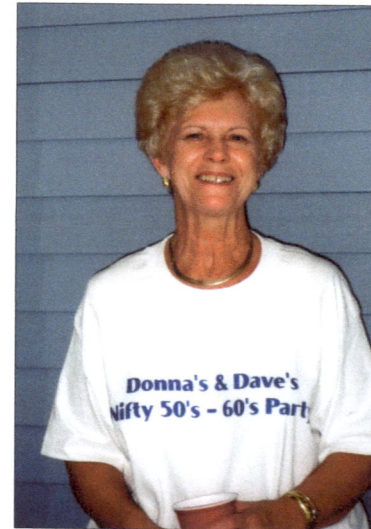

and Bill's widow, Doris Coats.

September 2006 reunion in Asheville, NC, near Biltmore Estate.
Left to right: Kathy, David, Doug, Deane, and Donna.

February 2013 reunion of the siblings at David's in Lake City.
Left to right: Donna, Doug, Deane, and David.

April 2016, Coats siblings plus Kathy at Gadsby's Tavern, Alexandria,
Virginia. Around the table, left foreground to right: Deane, Doug,
Donna, David, and Kathy.

L to R with birth order: Doug Coats - 3, Deane Dierksen - 1,
David Coats - 2, Donna Sevilla - 4. October 2018 reunion at the home
of Casey and Ellen Dameron in Summerville South Carolina.

BILL REMARRIES

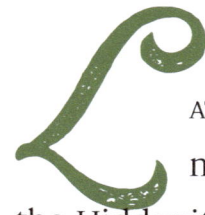

*L*ATER IN THE SAME YEAR that Ouida died, on 9 September 1982, Bill married Doris (Jolly) Wilborn in Taylorsville. Doris had worked at the Hiddenite plant prior to marrying Franklin Wilborn (1933-20 June 1981), who had also worked there.

*Wedding photo, Bill and Doris (Jolly) Wilborn Coats,
9 September 1982.*

Bill and Doris lived in Taylorsville, Statesville, and Taylorsville, N.C., again until his death 28 January 1994 from pneumonia and Alzheimer's disease. Their addresses, roughly:

- 1982-84 in Doris's house in Liledoun community, Taylorsville.

- 1984-85 for about two months, the Victoria Village house I visited on Hartness Road in Statesville late December 1984 or early January 1985. It was attached on the garage side to another home and had a great layout. They did not like it because it was across from the armory, and the music and parking were bad when there were performances there. Also, they said there was a park nearby used by blacks and many cut through their yard.

- 1985-89 at 1329 Radio Road Extension on Indian Ridge in Statesville. This is one Donna photographed. Doris remembers that I visited here once (though I don't recall it)—she said it was the time when she picked me up at Greensboro airport after a rough flight, and I was green at the gills! I do remember that part.

- 1989-ca. 1991, the house on the mountain in Taylorsville. Doris does not remember it being called Brushy Mountain. They lived in the bottom half of a large house owned by Harlen Robertson, on top of the mountain, with a spectacular view.

  After I sent out the photo of this house that Doris gave me, David commented in an email on 26 May 2007: "I noticed you had the mt. house labeled 'Bill Linney.' Although I was never there while they lived in it, Dad took me there a couple of times and I think Doris took me there once. I think Harlan Robertson owned it and lived in the upper or main part. It was up on a hill on the way to the Taylorsville radio station. Harlan is dead, but I saw and talked to his brother in 2001."

- 1991 (abt.)-1994, the house at 125 Northwood Circle, Taylorsville, where they lived when Bill died. It was a very nice house, fairly good-sized, and in a fairly new-looking, nice neighborhood.

By 1989, Bill had begun to show signs of memory loss— Doris probably noticed it before then. In summer 1989, they drove up to northern Virginia for a visit with my family and me. Their trip is easily dated from a four-generation photo of Bill, me, my daughter Marianne, and Marianne's son Luke, taken in my living room. But the trip wasn't so much memorable for what happened during the visit as for what happened on their way home. Bill had always had a wonderful sense of direction, could remember how to get to places he hadn't visited in years. On their return trip home, however, he got lost. I remembered that but didn't realize its significance at the time.

Four generations in summer 1989: Marianne (Dierksen) Fiorio and her son Luke, Bill, and me.

Several years later, some of us visited them in Taylorsville for Bill's birthday. I was there, Donna and Chuck were there, perhaps Doug, maybe David. Bill was very conservative in his political views, and we had all learned the hard way never to say a political word in his presence; sometimes he would bait us to start a political argument. So I cringed when Chuck—whose views are liberal—made a political statement.

To my amazement Bill didn't react. After Doris told us some time later of the Alzheimer diagnosis, I wondered why I hadn't put two and two together before then.

And then there is the bimbo statement. One time during this period Doug, Donna, and I were there. We wanted to go to Concord, but Bill did not. Doris was at work, and we couldn't leave him. So we made him go with us, and he wasn't too happy about that. On the way home, Doug was driving, Bill was in the front passenger seat, and Donna and I were in the back. As we got close to home, Bill looked at Doug and said they had to get rid of the bimbos in the back seat or his wife would be mad at him. That was both funny and not funny.

Bill continued to go downhill, had to give up driving, and wandered some on foot. Eventually, he had to have someone with him while Doris worked in the restaurant she owned. She was able to keep him at home almost to the end. Around the beginning of 1994, she felt she would have put into a nursing home, which he would have hated. Instead, he developed pneumonia and was hospitalized in Iredell Memorial Hospital in Statesville, where he died on 28 January 1994. Cause of death was pneumonia with Alzheimer's and prostate cancer as contributing conditions (per his death certificate).

Bill's obituary appeared in the Statesville (NC) Record, Sunday 28 January 1994:

BILL COATS, Sr.

TAYLORSVILLE—Mr. Louis David (Bill) Coats, Sr., 84, of 125 Northwood Circle, died Friday, Jan. 28, 1994 at Iredell Memorial Hospital. He had been seriously ill for five days.

Mr. Coats was born in Doland, S.D. on Jan. 15, 1910, a son of the late Ernest Leslie and Verona Paris Coats. He was educated in the Doland, S.D. schools and was the retired manager of a poultry production company. He was of the Protestant faith.

He was married to the former Doris Jolly, who survives.

Survivors, in addition to his wife, include two sons, Louis David Coats, Jr., of Orlando, Fla, and Douglas Coats of Carson City, Nev.; two daughters, Mrs. Deane Dierksen of Falls Church, Va. and Mrs. Donna Sevilla of San Diego,

Calif.; four brothers, Merle Coats of Rapid City, S.D., Frances [*sic*] Coats of Doland [S.D.], Ronald Coats of Verndale, Minn. and Maurice Costs [sic] of Virginia Beach, Va.; one sister, Mrs. Norma Thomas of Rapid City, S.D.; four stepchildren and six grandchildren and six great grandchildren.

Funeral services are scheduled for 2:30 p.m. today at Adams Funeral Home Chapel. Rev. David Boan will officiate. Burial will be in the Taylorsville City Cemetery.

The family will receive friends from 1:30-2:30 p.m. at Adams Funeral Home, and at other times, will assemble at the residence.

Memorials may be made to the Alzheimer's Foundation, North Carolina Southern Piedmont Chapter, 2001 Vail Ave., Charlotte, N.C., 28207.

We all felt that Doris had a halo because she had taken such good care of Bill through this illness. And he had not always been nice to her, either. But we all knew how lucky he was to have Doris, and how lucky we were that he had her. She was a natural caretaker and was and is a kind and thoughtful person.

ASSORTED MEMORIES OVER THE YEARS

THANKSGIVING MEMORIES:

My Thanksgiving memories are sketchy, with very few from Iowa. I don't remember ever having any relatives with us for Thanksgiving or any other holiday. I remember that Ouida made really good apple pie, but that is not necessarily a Thanksgiving memory. I also remember in grade school doing Thanksgiving art projects, featuring lots of turkeys and pilgrims, and singing "Over the River and Through the Woods to Grandmother's House We

Go." This and other holidays didn't seem to be a big deal. And maybe it wasn't just us. In her memoir of growing up in Ames, Iowa, at a slightly later date, author Susan Allen Toth said, "When I was growing up, Ames did not pay much attention to most holidays."[21]

From Concord, the memories are not good. For the first several years, we had a joint Thanksgiving with Alan and Kay Graves and their two children, alternating houses for the occasion. Alan also worked for Priebe, and they had moved to Concord about the same time we did. The joint dinners went on till one year, when it was at our house, and our dear papa didn't show up. I guess he didn't want to share Thanksgiving with them anymore—and he found a way to let everyone know. Talk about awkward!

From the 1960s, when my husband, Alan, and I went to the folks' house several times, I remember nonstop bridge games and generally a pretty good time. And from 1979, when Alan and I invited both sets of parents—his widowed father had remarried that year—I remember that Bill, who could be charming when he chose to, went out of his way to make things go smoothly when Herman Dierksen was acting like a total jerk. I also remember that no one came to help me clean up after Thanksgiving dinner—and that included my husband as well as my mother. I was so angry that when I finished cleaning up, I watched TV in the den while the rest of them lazed about the living room. In retrospect, maybe I was the lucky one. It took me a long time to realize that.

Doug remembers, "just a little from Iowa." He said, "Basically, I remember big dinners at the Kidd's and somebody else's house. Also, little tables for the kids and learning how to like green olives. Just good memories, not bad ones from Iowa. Concord was a mixed bag, but my overall impressions of Thanksgiving are warm and positive. Surprisingly, I just have the vaguest memories of Dad not showing up. Later on in Southern Pines mostly good memories of shared Thanksgivings with Marge and Vince Schweiger and family. Also some memories of Dad getting drunk. Strangely, very few memories of Thanksgivings in Roxboro and Hiddenite. Does that mean that the memories were bad and I suppressed them or [that the holidays were] just not memorable?"

Donna said, "Surprise, surprise. What I remember most is food related. I loved mother's pecan pie. The pumpkin pies were good, but the pecan pies were great. I also remember loving the mashed potatoes. My recollection is that mother always went to a lot of effort

---

21 Susan Allen Toth, *Blooming: A Small-Town Girlhood* (New York: Little, Brown and Company, 1981), 152.

at Thanksgiving not only with the food but also with the table. This was one of the few times the good dishes came out. I also recall thinking more than once that it was an awful lot of work for a pretty quick meal which usually was followed by the men heading off to watch TV (not that this was unique to that time, place, or family). As I was the only child at home during most of my youth, I recall Thanksgiving as a time when my siblings were likely to come home. Most of the Thanksgivings in my memory are from around the table at Hiddenite. Oddly enough, I don't have any remarkably vivid memories of particular Thanksgivings or events that occurred at any one Thanksgiving. It all sort of blurs together in my memory. I can picture Dad carving the turkey, which he did very well. In fact, even now, on the few occasions that Chuck gets asked to carve a poor turkey, I sort of grin because I know that Dad would be appalled at his lack of carving skills."

CHRISTMAS MEMORIES:

We always opened our presents on Christmas Eve, a tradition that came from Ouida's family. Doug remembers her saying that it was too cold in the "middle west" to open presents in the morning. Bill's brother Sid Coats told me a little about Christmas in the Coats household in S.D. when they were growing up: The kids all slept upstairs and would watch through the heat register on the floor on Christmas Eve to see if Santa would come. But the parents were on to them and never let the kids catch them putting presents out. Each child got one present, something to wear. Sid didn't know there wasn't a Santa Claus till he was about ten. They opened their presents on Christmas morning.

Donna said, "I always enjoyed Christmas Eve dinner and the opening of presents following when all of us were home. It is one of the few memories I have of all of us getting together, including Dad. I can remember Mother always insisting that the dishes had to be done and the kitchen cleaned before we could open presents. I cannot think of another family among my friends growing up who opened gifts on Christmas Eve; everyone else waited until Christmas morning."

In another message, Donna wrote: "Our family always opened gifts on Christmas Eve which was not the norm in North Carolina. We weren't the only ones with that custom, but most of my friends' families opened gifts on Christmas morning. The Christmas Eves that

I remember are the ones when my older brothers and sister came home. Mother made a special Christmas Eve meal, which was festive. Then we would have to get the dishes done before we could open gifts. I recall being very excited one year in Roxboro when I got a sled for Christmas. I also recall many years, though not every year, when mother would make oyster stew. I thought of that on Christmas Eve this year [2003] when I was at the market and saw oysters prominently featured in a holiday food display. I recall that I never wanted to try the oysters. . . [I only wanted to] drink the buttered milk and eat the crackers. Every once in a while, I run across someone who mentions having oyster stew on Christmas Eve, and I feel a connection. I suspect that is a regional custom."

Deane: I have no recollection of oyster stew at Christmas, but that may be because I (and maybe my brothers as well) refused even to drink the milk that it was cooked in. Perhaps the folks waited until I was grown and gone to add it to the Christmas Eve menu. Or perhaps it was a new custom adopted after they moved south.

Earlier, when any of us still believed in Santa, Bill would take us out to look at Christmas decorations around town while Ouida was doing the dishes after Christmas Eve dinner. Amazingly enough, Santa always came while we were out. Imagine the coincidence of that happening every year!! And imagine that Ouida never caught him in the act. I have a vague memory of hearing Santa Claus in 1941 when we lived in St. Paul. We lived in a duplex, and the husband in the couple next door acted as Santa. I am not sure whether I actually remember this or remember Ouida telling me about it. The neighbors were Jewish, but the man was happy to do this.

CHRISTMAS GIFTS:

I have practically no memories about what I got for Christmas as a kid. The one exception is the year I was in about 5th grade when David and I both got our first bicycles. Doug got some kind of vehicular toy, perhaps a pedal airplane. This was the first year that bikes, etc., were available after World War II. I have no recollection of being either happy or unhappy about the gifts. I do recall that the presents Santa brought the Coats children were not gift-wrapped. Ouida said Santa had too many places to go to have time to wrap presents for children.

We also got gifts from relatives. The Coats clan drew names for gifts for kids; the adults didn't exchange gifts. Again, I don't recall what I might have gotten. I do remember that Ouida left the all the gifts that came in the mail in the mailing box till Christmas Eve, and I always wanted her to open it up so we could see the wrapped packages. Our Moulton grandparents always sent gifts, but I think they were small ones. I seem to remember getting books from them. Two that came from them, probably at Christmas, were *Silas Marner* (paperback) and one by Storm Jamieson, a fiction writer that Grandpa Moulton was quite fond of. These probably date from my junior high years.

Several times in Concord every present under the tree was wrapped in the same pattern of wrapping paper. (By this time, no one in the house still believed in Santa.) Bill was given big rolls of paper from some vendor (Dixie paper?), and Ouida used it up. This was an example, as she used to say, "of my old Scotch heart." I just hated seeing everything with the same paper and complained quite a bit about it.

In Southern Pines we all got together one year to get Dad a tuxedo as a surprise Christmas gift. He made sure we all knew it wasn't a surprise. Donna commented that the "only present that I remember getting Dad that I think was a big hit was the Polaroid camera."

David's said his first Christmas memories are "in Perry, in a big old house on the edge of town (I think before 708 First St.). I remember the upstairs, and Dad taking us out at just the wrong time so we missed Santa. Biggest memory of that era is at 708 when Deane and I got bikes. The weather was very fair, and I remember trying to ride around the block and falling off repeatedly as I learned. (I still fall a lot). Don't have many memories from Concord but do remember Hiddenite when I was in the Navy. The "homecoming" events were nicely capped off by the memory of Deane and Alan one year and Alan's secret drink—Scarlet O'Hara. I remember taking him to another county to buy the booze (Southern Comfort, which has alternately been called the fine southern lady and the booze that gave rot gut a bad name). I still have and display the family pictures of that visit. Everyone looks pretty good in the pictures, so I can only assume they were taken before the special drinks. I doubt Doug or Dad had many memories of that evening. I don't remember much about the candies except the caramel. [They were] always my favorites, and I just remember Mom's 'Xmas Candies.' She even sent me some when I was overseas. I never did understand the gifts on Xmas Eve vs. Xmas Morn. [In my] family [with my kids]. . . we've never done that. . . we just had the couple of special gifts available to kids first thing Xmas Morn, then we waited for whatever family was around, had breakfast with everyone and then opened presents."

Just for the record, the basic ingredients for Scarlett O'Haras are Southern Comfort and cranberry juice. After getting David's message above, I asked Alan if he remembered that occasion. He remembered one where he "was drinking Screwdrivers while I watched football games with your father. That was the one where everybody else sat down for Thanksgiving dinner, and later on I had a bowl of oatmeal. I remember standing in the bedroom and Donna came back to use the bathroom and saw me standing in the room with no lights on and just leaning against the wall. She asked me what I was doing, and I told her I was watching the hot air coming out of the floor duct. She muttered a groan of disgust and went into the bathroom."

I do not recall when we put up our Christmas tree or anything much about the decorations, except that we always took it down the day after Christmas. I know we put icicles on the tree and that the lightstrings we used then were such that if one light went out the whole string went out. It was always a big hassle to find and replace the bad bulb. Also, I don't think we ever had Christmas stockings. I think Ouida thought it was too much trouble and too hard to fill them.

Ouida's Christmas candies were memorable for us and for our grade-school teachers. I think she did this until we were grown. Donna said, "My most favorite memory of the Christmas season was mother making candy. She would make batches of fudge, caramels, divinity, penuche, and date nut candy and then make up tins or boxes of the candy for us to give to teachers. The caramels were my favorite. I remember that old black pot with the warped bottom, which I can still visualize perfectly. When mother thought the caramels were done cooking, she would take it off the stove, put a towel in her lap, and start beating. She always said the secret was not to overcook the caramels to keep them from sugaring and to beat the heck out of them. Quite a few years in a row, she and I made candy on the weekend when the networks were broadcasting the *Wizard of Oz*. I'm not sure why that movie was a holiday broadcast, but anytime I see a reference to it, I think of mother and making candy."

Deane: Donna and I tried our hand at the caramel recipe at Christmas 1968. Our caramels were delicious if you didn't mind eating them with a spoon!

David remembers that pot. He said, "It was cast aluminum with a warped bottom from overheating and black around the sides from use. I don't remember the lid, but I know there was one because it was the same pot that Dad used to make popcorn (after which he would melt butter in it). The pot ought to be framed or at least bronzed, but I'm sure it went the way of most things after Mom's death. It is probably the only kitchen implement that I remember. I also remember for years trying to find a pot that would do popcorn as well. I never did, and although I like and eat the microwave popcorn, it cannot match the pot and the 'Jolly Time' white popcorn of our tainted youth."

None of us seems to remember any other traditions or attending church programs. I recall that we never went away at Christmas and never had any relatives with us when I was a kid.

COATS RADIO AND TV PROGRAMS, 1940S & AFTER.

Radio programs Ouida and Bill liked:

- Ouida always listened in the morning to the *Breakfast Club* with Don McNeil. That was a favorite for years. McNeil had a march played every morning, and I used to march around the kitchen to it in Perry. This program was still on into the 1950s and perhaps beyond.

- Both parents, but especially Ouida, listened to all the mystery shows on in the evening. *Mr. Keene, Tracer of Lost Persons*; *The Shadow* ("Who knows what evil lurks in the hearts of man. . . the Shadow knows"); and I think some others. Perhaps one was about Mr. Campion. Another was about a couple that was always solving mysteries: *Mr. and Mrs. North*.

- Fred Waring and the Pennsylvanians. Ouida thought they were a wonderful singing group. I doubt if Bill paid any attention to this one!

- *The Bing Crosby Show*. Ouida was a big fan, but I don't know how Bill felt.

- *The Lone Ranger*. Bill was a tremendous fan, and it wasn't advisable to interrupt while this show was on the radio. It was a staple of my childhood, on three nights a week at 6:30 p.m. Brace Beemer played the lead role—he had a very distinctive voice. One commentator said that "No other old time radio western has influenced American culture like the *Lone Ranger*. From the first broadcast in 1933, to the first movie serial in 1938, to the television program in 1949, the Lone Ranger has been a part of the myths created about the Western United States. The Lone Ranger has created a great part of the mystique of the Wild West with his pursuit of justice on his white horse, Silver, and his trademark silver bullets. *The Lone Ranger* began as a humble radio show and has become a legend of American popular culture."[22] Hi Ho, Silver!

- Comedy shows: *The Fred Allen Show*; *The Jack Benny Program*; *The Phil Harris-Alice Faye Show* (Phil Harris always ended the show with a long patter song that ended with "That's what I like about the South"); *The Bob Hope Show*; *Fibber McGee and Molly*, who lived at 69 Wistful Vista; *The Bickersons* with Don Ameche and Frances Langford; *The Charlie McCarthy Show* with Edgar Bergen; *The Great Gildersleeve*; *The George Burns and Gracie Allen Show*. One or both parents listened to these. One I particularly remember that Ouida did not like was *Amos 'n' Andy*.

Television programs. We got our first television set when we moved to Concord in 1951 and were all "videots" for a while! Radio pretty much became a thing of the past. We got only three or four television channels then. Some of our favorite shows were:

- *Arthur Godfrey and His Friends* (later simply *The Arthur Godfrey Show)*, broadcast 1949-1959. It was a morning show and a very big deal when I was in high school. People either liked him or hated him! Ouida got a big kick out of it. My high school English teacher thought it was awful.

- *The Jack Paar Tonight Show*, 1957-1962. I think Ouida also watched the hosts who took over when Paar quit. I doubt if Bill was ever awake to watch this one.

---

22 Robert Wheadon, online 11 September 2004, at http://gaga.essortment.com/lonerangerradi_rlmb.htm.

- *The Fred Waring Show* with Fred Warning and His Pennsylvanians had a weekly choral music show (1949-1955) and periodic specials after that. Ouida loved this one.

- Colgate Comedy Hour, broadcast from 1950 to 1955 on Sunday nights. Rotating hosts were Eddie Cantor, Jimmy Durante, Martin and Lewis, Fred Allen, Gordon MacRae, Abbott & Costello, Donald O'Connor. The whole family watched this show.

- *I Love Lucy* and its many successors.

- Sports. Bill watched any and all.

- *Peter Gunn* (1958-1961). Donna is sure that Bill "saw every episode of that series more than once."

- *Gunsmoke*, which ran on television from 1955 to1975. There was also a radio version. Donna doubts Bill stayed up late enough to watch this one, but someone in the household did. I saw quite a few episodes myself.

- *The Jack Benny Program*, on television from 1950 to 1965.

- *Your Hit Parade*, on television from 1950 to 1959 and on the radio before that. I watched this religiously when I was in high school. Two of the lead singers were Snooky Lanson and Dorothy Collins. I couldn't wait to find out what was Number One, although often there was no suspense about that!

- *The Ed Sullivan Show*, televised from 1948 to 1971.

- The Lawrence Welk Show, 1955-1982 (and in reruns forever!). One reason Ouida liked this show was nostalgia. Welk and his band had played around South Dakota when she and Bill were courting. She said that then when Welk was playing, people thought it was nothing special, just Lawrence Welk!

- *What's My Line?* (1950-1967). Shown on Sunday nights about 10 p.m., it featured celebrity panelists who had to guess each guest's occupation, most of which were unusual in some way. Ouida loved it and so did I. The host was John Daly. There was a variety of panelists but I mostly remember Bennet Cerf, Dorothy Kilgallen, and Arlene Francis.

It seemed that Bill could go to sleep in front of any television program. We used to say that he exercised his taste by going to sleep. One sure way to wake him up was to change the channel or turn it off. Worked every time!

FAMILY READING MATERIAL WHEN I WAS A KID

As mentioned earlier, Ouida was a big reader. She frequently said that the three things you did right away when you moved to a new town were: subscribe to the newspaper, register to vote, and get a library card. Most of the books we had were library books—I don't remember anyone buying many books, except the *Readers' Digest Condensed Books*, probably dating from the Concord years. Paperback books were not nearly as prevalent then as they are today. We did, however, have lots of magazines around the house. And when the new issues arrived, all else except meals had to wait while Ouida read them.

From the Hiddenite years Donna said she remembers Ouida "sitting in her rocking chair (whatever happened to that chair?) and reading most evenings. I do not remember what books she was reading. I really couldn't say whether they were mysteries, fiction, classics, biographies, or some eclectic mixture. I do know that she and I made regular trips to the library in Statesville every week since Alexander County did not have a library." I remember that she read mysteries by the dozens and several times remarked that when she had read all the mysteries in the local library, it was time to move.

My visit some years ago to a Norman Rockwell exhibit at Corcoran Gallery reminded me of one magazine that loomed large in our household: *The Saturday Evening Post*. The exhibit included a display of all his covers for the *Post*, many of which I remembered. This was a weekly that we got from the time I was old enough to remember to at least until I left home. Ouida read it religiously, and I think I did, too. It had continued stories, short stories, and lots of articles. I have forgotten most of them but do remember that there were frequently serial novels by Clarence Buddington Kelland. Ouida didn't think much of him as an author, but I read all his stuff, which was mostly mystery thriller type. Only one scene has stuck in my mind: The male villain, who was probably about to seduce or rape the heroine, died when the mirror he had mounted on the ceiling over his bed fell and a piece from it stabbed him in the heart.

Ouida didn't care much for *Life* or *Look* magazines, though we may have gotten the latter for a while. *Collier's* was also around. Other magazines included *Readers' Digest*, which I think all of us looked at. I know I read most of the articles as well as all the little short human interest and humorous items, a few of which I can still recall. *Readers' Digest* was much different then and had some substance to it. Several magazines with mystery stories were also on the subscription list. One was an anthology called *Ellery Queen's Mystery Magazine*. I think there was at least one more.

Most of the other magazines I remember were women's magazines: *Ladies' Home Journal*, *Woman's Home Companion*, *McCall's*, *Redbook,* and another magazine that was similar to it (title may be *American*), and *Cosmopolitan* (which was very different then than after Helen Gurley Brown took it over). For some reason, Ouida didn't like *Good Housekeeping*, and I don't think we got it.

Betty Friendan's 1963 book, *The Feminine Mystique,* caused us to reevaluate the content of the women's magazines. In it Friedan described the "problem that had no name"—women who were unhappy with the idea that being solely a housewife and mother was their main role and source of satisfaction. Freidan cited many articles in women's magazines that reinforced that role. When I read the book I actually remembered many of those articles in some detail. After Ouida read it she said she felt as if she had been sold down the river.

The magazines included biographical articles and book excerpts and serializations. One was the serialization of the autobiography by Consuela Vanderbilt Balsan, titled *The Glitter and the Gold*. A Vanderbilt daughter, she was an American heiress who was basically sold as a bride to the Duke of Marlborough, whom she later divorced (a really big deal then). She had a happy second marriage. Another book excerpt was about a woman alone in a cabin in Alaska during a blizzard with a critically ill baby for whom she could do nothing but hold him. I think the baby survived.

I remember reading some periodicals that had very graphic and detailed information, including lots of photos, about the Holocaust. This was around the time of the Nuremberg Trials and before we left Perry when I was 13. One Nazi atrocity that sticks in my mind is a description of using human skin for lampshades. There are some others, too. Some were news articles; some were first-person accounts.

I haven't looked at old issues of any of these magazines in years, but a while back ran across an interesting comment about them in a memoir by Susan Jacoby. Ms. Jacoby wrote, "In spite of their shortcomings nearly all of the general-interest magazines of the fifties offered, to readers of all ages, a staggering amount of serious information, especially when compared to the celebrity mad publications of the nineties."[23] This comment would probably apply to the magazines of the 1940s as well.

We also got several children's magazines, such as *Children's Playmate* and *Jack & Jill.* One or perhaps both had continuing stories that I just loved. I remember saving up all the installments so I could read them at the same time and not have to wait for the next chapter. Doug recalls that he and David got *Boys' Life.* The Girl Scout magazine then was called *American Girl,* and I got that.

While I don't remember Bill ever reading anything besides the newspaper (mostly the sports page) or an occasional sports magazine, Donna recalls that he got *Sports Illustrated* and *Business Week*. He also looked at *New Yorker*. Whether he did more than look at the cartoons, Donna didn't know, but he regularly did at least that. The differences in perception here no doubt result from the different timeframes each of us would remember and the number of people in the household. One comment Bill made to me many times about reading was that you should always read the preface first.

---

23 Susan Jacoby, *Half-Jew: A Daughter's Search for Her Family's Buried Past* (New York: Scribner's, 2000), 187.